P9-BZJ-398

P9-BZJ-398

THE ART OF
DRIED FLOWERS

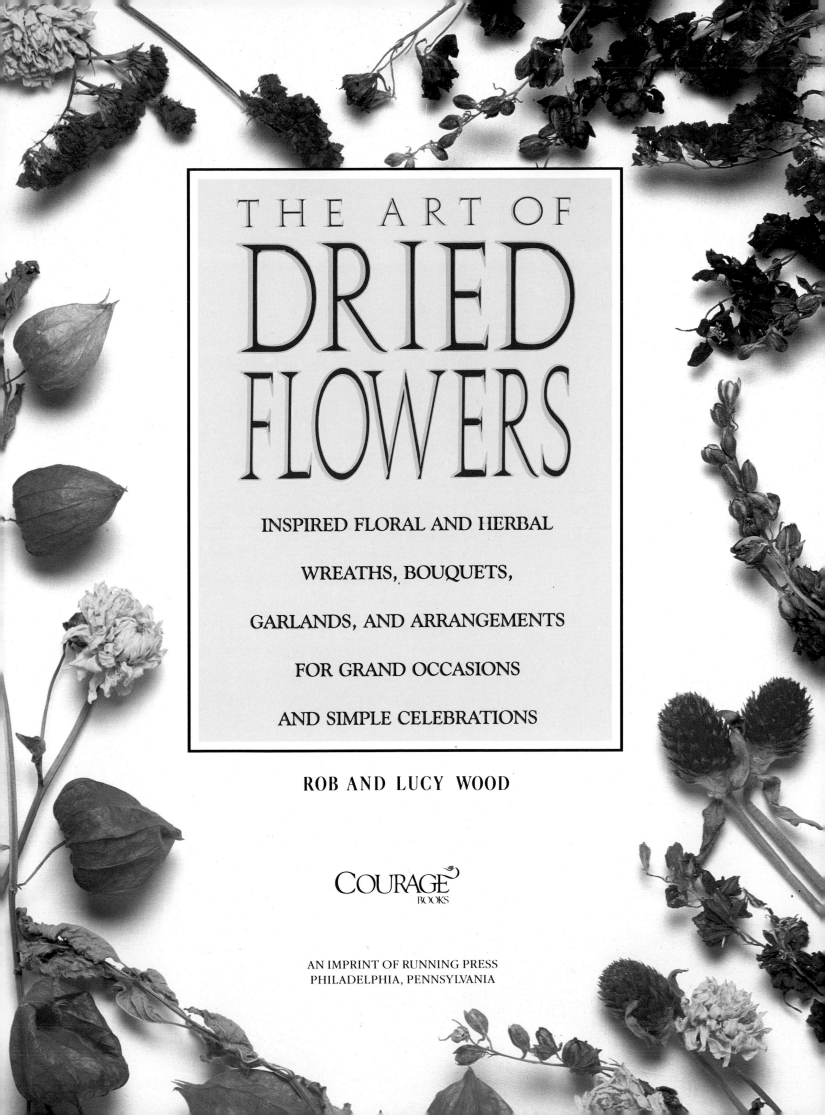

THE ART OF
DRIED
FLOWERS

INSPIRED FLORAL AND HERBAL

WREATHS, BOUQUETS,

GARLANDS, AND ARRANGEMENTS

FOR GRAND OCCASIONS

AND SIMPLE CELEBRATIONS

ROB AND LUCY WOOD

COURAGE
BOOKS

AN IMPRINT OF RUNNING PRESS
PHILADELPHIA, PENNSYLVANIA

A RUNNING PRESS/FRIEDMAN GROUP BOOK

Copyright © 1991, 1992 by Running Press Book Publishers and Michael Friedman Publishing Group, Inc.

9 8 7 6 5 4 3 2 1

Digit on the right indicates the number of this printing.

ISBN 1-56138-168-3

THE ART OF DRIED FLOWERS
Inspired Floral and Herbal Wreaths, Bouquets, Garlands, and Arrangements for
Grand Occasions and Simple Celebrations
was prepared and produced by
Michael Friedman Publishing Group, Inc.
15 West 26th Street
New York, New York 10010

Editor: Melissa Schwarz
Art Director: Jeff Batzli
Designer: Devorah Levinrad
Photography Editor: Christopher Bain

Typeset by Classic Type, Inc.
Color separations by Excel Graphic Arts Co.
Printed in Hong Kong by Leefung-Asco Printers Ltd.

Published by Courage Books
An imprint of Running Press
125 South Twenty-second Street
Philadelphia, Pennsylvania 19103

ACKNOWLEDGEMENTS

We are especially grateful to the following persons for allowing us to use their lovely settings and props for photographs in this book: Ron Cubbison of Boxwood Farm, Hanover, Pennsylvania; Bob Pitman and Martha Amereihn of Crowsfoot, White Hall, Maryland; Sheila and Babu Rao, Pikesville, Maryland; and Lena Caron of Ladew Topiary Gardens of Monkton, Maryland, one of the finest public topiary gardens in America.

Thanks are also due the following:

The staff and photographers of the Michael Friedman Publishing Group with whom we experienced an especially amicable relationship. Special thanks are due Melissa Schwarz, our editor; Christopher Bain, photography editor; Bill Seitz, principal photographer for the project; and freelance photographers Sharon Gynup and Peggy Fox.

Maureen Beuhrle and the International Herb Growers and Marketers Association for introducing us to a remarkable network of people who combine love of plants with earning a living. Some of the finest people we've met are Betsy and Ned Williams, Janet Walker, Pat Reppert, and Margot and Jim Forcier-Call.

Ralph Cramer of Cramer's Posie Patch and Ruth Watson, Lucy's cousin, who gave critical initial encouragement and technical advice.

Emmanuel Episcopal Church, the scene of our first wreath-making workshop, after which we turned to each other and said, "Shall we do this for the rest of our lives?" Emmanuel was also the first place our work was shown and continues to be a place of friendship and inspiration.

Pam and Gould Charshee and Amy Swisher for lending back our work for inclusion in the book. Jim Joyner for providing the splendid Scottish brooch.

Harriet Flotte for generously sharing with us her techniques for silica drying and some marvelous peonies, roses, and dahlias, dried to perfection. Raymond A. Fleck Inc. for providing the silica gel. Peggy Kirkpatrick for showing us how to make sliced apple wreaths.

W.F.K. Seymour and his superb fantail willows; Buck Godwin of Alberta Supernaturals; Rene Piper of the New Englander; and Nancy Herbst of Mountain Farms, Inc., for cooperation far exceeding expectations in supplying us with rich troves of unusual dried materials.

Josh Fendell and Craft Concepts for lending important props used in several of the arrangement settings. And Ann Forret for invaluable tips about Scottish flora.

Carol Huettner and Doris Rill for exceptional typing and computer skills in preparing the manuscript for editing.

Sue Chlumsky, Peggy Fellerath, Gail Mitchell, Betty Sifleet, Marlene Twilley, and Dorothy Ward, who helped us keep pace with wholesale and retail orders while we were distracted with book writing.

Our special friend, the late professor Robert Lewis Baker, who was so sensitive to the aesthetic nuances of the plant kingdom.

Thomas Jefferson and St. Francis for being ongoing inspirations in our lives.

TABLE OF CONTENTS

AN INFORMAL
BOUQUET OF
FLOWERS DRIED JUST AS THEY
WERE GATHERED CAN BE
CHARMING.

INTRODUCTION

Long before meeting Rob, like so many other children, I picked and carried home bouquets of all sorts for my very special mother. Depending upon the season, there were dandelions and violets, possibly accompanied by the delicate trumpets of pale lavender flowers from the princess tree, or Queen Anne's lace and goldenrod, forming a taller, more airy and graceful offering. My family had only a tiny yard with fragile crocuses for only a week in spring and pussy-cat-faced pansies I delighted in tending. Therefore, what flowers were available to me for indoor enjoyment were from the woods or park, often wild, sometimes known as "weed" by those with an uncurious eye. But those city pickings had great beauty to my open eyes and heart.

As a young adult I owned and restored an elegant Victorian townhouse. Its twenty-square-foot (two-square-meter) courtyard garden housed a formal oval fish pool framed by evergreen shrubs and vines, which provided color and an interesting texture all year. Crepe myrtle contributed a rich raspberry foam of flowers, but these were enjoyed more on the tree than on the table. As there were no flowers for cutting, one afternoon, in anticipation of dinner with our friend the horticulture professor, I went scouting along the alley behind the house. Waiting to be gathered there were pearly-white clematis on trailing vines, starry Queen Anne's lace, pale-yellow goldenrod, and the sharp blue of chicory for a cooling accent. The resulting arrangement was charming in its simplicity, just suited to a lighthearted visit with old friends on a breezy porch over a long, lingering dinner.

Later I lived in a tiny cottage by a river. Again I loved bringing the outdoors in. Wild milkweed flowers and their pods, lined with silky-threaded seeds, old friend Queen Anne's lace, and the brilliant orange of butterfly weed (a close relative of milkweed), came from the roadside. From the shrubs and gardens around the cottage, hydrangea blossoms and gently scented herbs became my joy. Some of these I discovered also dried well, becoming a bounty of flowers for wintertime. Over the years since I left that cozy home, my delight in the magic of planting, growing, and preserving flowers has grown along with my husband's and my knowledge and experience.

A WORLD OF MULTIPLE HUES OFFERS ABUNDANT OPPORTUNITIES FOR AN IMAGINATIVE ARRANGER.

The lessons of those early days continue to hold true for us: The simplest of materials, carefully chosen for time, place, and person, can yield the most effective and personal results. This is a focus we wish to share in this book of ideas for arranging dried flowers and herbs.

We will share with you our joy in discovering flowers, leaves, and branches of varied forms, colors, textures, and scents. In the first chapter we discuss finding and gathering materials from garden, roadside, and field. Here you will find tips on harvesting different flowers and drying techniques.

In chapter two we introduce our approach to choosing and using flowers in ways that uniquely honor a specific person, place, or event for which they are intended. Consideration is given to containers and to the forms an arrangement can take and how these may enhance the "meaning" of the arrangement.

Chapters three, four, five, and six provide numerous examples of arrangements, each with a discussion of its special purpose, the reasons for the flowers chosen, and how the design developed. In chapter three are arrangements for occasions or events, while in chapter four our

MANY FLOWERS
GROWN IN THE
GARDEN OR GATHERED IN THE
FIELD CAN BE HANG-DRIED.

inspirations derive from places we've visited or cultures and periods in history that intrigue us. Each arrangement in chapter five was designed for a specific location, some grand, some intimate, some traditional, some modern. Special people provide the impetus for the arrangements in chapter six. In the discussion of each arrangement we share our thinking, the underlying reasoning behind the decisions made. These are not intended to be prescriptions; rather they are examples of ways of thinking with flowers, form, color, and texture. We hope you will feel free to develop ideas of your own.

Techniques basic to the designs in this book are illustrated in chapter seven. None of these are especially difficult, although some become easier with practice. Most of the techniques are useful for a variety of designs, thus as you experiment and work with flowers, your skill will develop over time.

Our hope is that this book will encourage you to go beyond the tried and true (and expected), to develop your own imagination, and to be increasingly sensitive to the myriad possibilities for using flowers in your life and your environment.

FLOWERS GROWN IN
THE SUMMER SUN
CAN LAST MANY SEASONS IF
PROPERLY DRIED.

❧1❧

GATHERING AND PRESERVING FLOWERS

Many arrangements begin months earlier as we let our eyes wander through the garden, along the roadside, and into the fields and woods, and discover the myriad treasures waiting for an inquisitive eye to recognize their possibilities. Gathering flowers and leaves in a multitude of colors, textures, and forms will yield rich choices for future creative work.

Once collected, each flower is dried according to its own needs. Many are bunched to hang in a dry, dark, warm, yet airy attic. Others are gently laid flat on a screen. Some flowers warrant being carefully buried in a bed of silica gel, which removes moisture while supporting the flower's structure, while leaves can often be pressed flat between layers of absorbant paper. The drying method is chosen to complement the floral material, resulting in a beauty that preserves the unique quality of each flower.

GETTING TO KNOW YOUR PLANTS

By far the best source of materials for drying and arranging is your immediate surroundings. When we moved to Spoutwood Farm in 1983, we inherited a number of hosta plants in a shaded flower bed. It took several years before the ample, pointed, fan-shaped leaves suggested themselves for pressing, yielding fine green and yellow additions to large-scale arrangements. Similarly, we became beneficiaries of a bountiful crop of tiny cones from a grove of hemlock planted as a wind screen long before our arrival. River birches that we introduced along our streams for erosion control produce a wealth of chartreuse-tinged greenery, as does the *Lonicera fragrantissima* with its dark green, easy-to-press leaves. From our perennial borders come iris, lilies, and roses to dry with silica. This year we are hoping to try drying whole branchlets of our deutzia shrub to utilize its profusion of fairy-white flowers. In the cutting gardens are the truly everlasting strawflowers, our first real planted harvest, their abundant colors requiring almost daily plucking.

RED PLUME CELOSIA (FAR LEFT) AND BLUE SALVIA ARE TWO OF THE FLOWERS WE GROW IN OUR GARDEN FOR THEIR BRILLIANT DRIED COLOR AND CONTRASTING TEXTURES.

GRASSES AND
GRAINS YIELD A
VARIETY OF INTERESTING
TEXTURES.

GLOBE AMARANTH
AND CELOSIA
AWAITING HARVEST IN THE FIELD
(OPPOSITE PAGE).

Many a time we are lured to run our fingers over their characteristically crisp petals. Nigella, also known as love-in-a-mist, is a pleaser all along its life cycle. The "mist" is first observed as a lacy-green enfoldment guarding delicate white, blue, or pink flowers that lingers on to oversee development of the miraculous maroon-striped pods. Arranging flowers in the best of all possible worlds starts with moments like these, getting to know your own plants as they grow in your garden or landscape.

Anyone with the slightest interest in working with dried flowers and herbs sooner or later begins to discover the legions of plants that liberally spread across natural landscapes. Travels about the countryside quickly become field-scanning and plant-gathering missions. In almost any area, roadsides, fields, and woods offer a wealth of textures and colors. Recently we were driving not far from home when we noticed an uncharacteristic blue cast in an upcoming field of wheat. Closer inspection revealed wild bachelor's buttons, *Centaurea cyanus,* successfully outstretching the wheat to display their azure crowns. The farmer allowed us to remove a large supply of stemmed blossoms, as long as we didn't trample his wheat. On another occasion, it was wheat itself that surprised us, a simple delicately awned variety, which had spilled over into a ditch, appearing to all as a roadside weed. That lightly bearded find showed up in many a wreath and arrangement that year.

When gathering from the wild, it is important to ask questions. Always ask yourself first whether removing a portion of the plant in question will jeopardize the plant's survival. We would never remove the blazing orange butterfly weed, *Asclepias tuberosa,* sometimes called Indian paintbrush and pleurisy root, from its hard-won positions along sunny hillsides in our area; it is too scarce. We would rather cultivate it at home. Prolific stands of goldenrod, on the other hand, can withstand judicious thinning.

Another question, "Would you mind...?", is an essential matter of courtesy, and should always be directed whenever possible to the owner of the land from which you intend to remove plant matter.

As you carefully observe your own plants and nature's bounty beyond the garden, you will inevitably start seeing in a new way. You will see wondrous shades of colors, textures soft and prickly, shapes fanciful and uniform. We never tire of growing globe amaranth plants; something

makes us like to be around these color factories. From midsummer until frost their cloverlike heads, hundreds to a plant, sparkle with enthusiastic richness: white, pink, lavender, delicious red, purple, hot pink, orange, and even peach. Red is a difficult color to capture dried, but two of our favorite reds come from well-drained fields and roadsides: the spectacular dark-red berry-spires of sumac, and wild rose hips, which dry on the bush over the winter (if the birds don't get them first). This year we discovered one such multiflora rose bush with hips four times normal size—a wonderful find. We are ever on the lookout for fields of Queen Anne's lace. To retain their starry snowflake quality, we pluck the heads and dry them face down, sometimes two or three thick on a screen in the heat of our chicken barn attic. But we don't know whether we like the lacy snowflake stage or the later bird's nest phase, when the outstretched bloom starts curving back on itself to form a fistlike trove of seed, better. (By the way, if you're looking for a plant similar in texture

DRIED

STRAWFLOWERS AND

GLOBE AMARANTH READY TO

USE IN WREATHS.

to Queen Anne's lace, that blooms much earlier, consider the wild form of yarrow with its delicate fernlike leaves and dusty white cauliflower florets.)

Both growing your own plants and gathering from nature are good ways to get material for your dried creations, but you may want to supplement these methods with two others—buying from or trading with other growers and suppliers, and drying material purchased from florists. We seem to be unable to survive without the bubbly effervescence of pepperberries, which grow only in climates far warmer than ours. We buy them through the mail from growers or wildcrafters in California or South America. Our greatest Valentine's gift ever was from Rob's brother's family in California—a sizable "care package" containing an incredible stash of fresh picked pepperberries. We also buy annual statice, or *Statice sinuata,* which, with its tufted texture and vibrant colors, also seems to grow better in California.

The list of sources in the back of the book includes some dried flower suppliers. Band together with friends to buy wholesale, or look for the retail outlets in your area.

It also helps to befriend your local florist, wholesale or retail. We like the rocketlike purple spires of *Liatris spicata* so well that we harvest them from our own garden in midsummer and buy them from the florist when we run out. Florists are often a reliable source of bells of Ireland, many kinds of eucalyptus, and mimosa branches for hang drying; roses, irises, and carnations for silica drying; and all manner of leaves and ferns for pressing.

One final word on learning about the suitability of materials for drying. Perhaps our greatest ally in this regard is our native curiosity and willingness to experiment. In our home all available hooks, pegs, racks, and lighting fixtures quickly become festooned with experiments in drying. In our chicken barn we tried to give in to the inevitable by placing scores of old-fashioned nails along the exposed beams. Within one growing season they were all occupied. So, when you plan places to hang your botanical discoveries, be generous. You might also want to label your finds. Many a time we have returned to our transformed treasure, only to discover that we couldn't remember for the life of us what it was or where it came from.

ROSES, MARIGOLDS, BOTTLE BRUSH, AND CHINESE LANTERNS, AMONG OTHERS—ALL HANG-DRIED TO SAVE THEIR BRILLIANT TONES OF RED AND ORANGE.

HARVESTING AND DRYING

When it comes to harvesting, each plant has its own needs, often more subtle than rule-of-thumb guidelines. Some prolific producers, like ammobium and strawflowers, can be harvested as often as every day in the height of the season. Cornflower, or bachelor's button, requires considerable attention. Unless it is harvested the same day the buds open and then quickly dried, faded color and falling petals are apt to result. On the other hand, globe amaranth and celosia maintain picking color for several weeks, allowing more flexibility during harvest time. Some flowers, especially tall spiked ones like liatris, larkspur, and annual statice, mature unevenly along the stem. The latter two bloom from the bottom up and are harvestable when three-quarters (or more) of the flowers are open. Waiting too long allows unsightly deterioration of the lower flowers. In contrast, liatris blooms in just the opposite manner (that is, from the top down), and should be picked when the top inch or two (2.5-5 cm) are in full glory. If you wait too long, the tips of the blooms will shatter and their color will darken.

While gaining experience with particular plants, there are some general principles to keep in mind. Flowers maintain color best when picked at or just before their blooming peak and then quickly dried. Harvesting after dew or rain has thoroughly evaporated is as important to this process as is stripping off leaves. The drying time for Queen Anne's lace and globe amaranth, if they are to be used exclusively for wreath work, is reduced significantly by taking the heads only. Flowers already harvested should be kept as fresh as possible until they are dried. Some flowers can be left in the shade in ample baskets until drying, while others, especially those to be silica-dried, ought to be kept in a bucket of water also in the shade.

BITTERSWEET, SUMAC, PEPPERBERRIES, AND BOUGAINVILLEA ARE AMONG THE TREES AND VINES PRODUCING TREASURES FOR DRIED FLORAL WORK.

PURPLE GLOBE AMARANTH MAKES A LOVELY GARDEN DISPLAY AS WELL AS AN ENDURING DRIED FLOWER (OPPOSITE PAGE).

THE FLOWER
BRANCHES ABOVE
ARE DRYING IN THE WARMTH
AND DARKNESS OF OUR CHICKEN
BARN ATTIC.

LONG STEMS OF
COCKSCOMB
CAREFULLY HUNG TO DRY
(OPPOSITE PAGE, TOP).

AIR-DRYING

At Spoutwood we use three drying techniques: air-drying, pressing, and silica gel-drying. Of these, the simplest and most natural is air-drying. The most common method of air-drying is to hang bunches of material. Flowers that do well with this method include yarrow, nigella, plumed celosia, statice, larkspur, tansy, chives, roses, sea holly, hydrangea, blue salvia, bee balm, and lamb's ears. Bunches are bound together with a rubber band and suspended upside down in a dark, dry, warm, well-ventilated area. Attics are commonly employed for air-drying, but most places with good air circulation and a minimum of sunlight and moisture will do. Plant material not suitable for hanging, such as strawflower and Queen Anne's lace heads, as well as pods and cones, can be dried in the same places on layers of wood, cardboard, or screens. Grasses and grains often dry well upright.

Drying times vary according to the type of plant material and the drying conditions. In summertime in the heat of our tin-roofed attic, fast-drying flowers like Queen Anne's lace may take only several days, while moisture-laden celosia heads may require three or more weeks if not broken apart. For the slower-drying flowers, it is essential to ensure good ventilation. We have used a variety of fans for such occasions.

We also use our neighbor Ralph Cramer's unique system of tiered racks, designed to support bunches on long wood slats or flower heads on screens. There are many ways to hang bunches, such as ropes, wires, chains, hooks, coat hangers, or drying racks. The old-fashioned collapsible clothes-drying racks are ideal and look beautiful covered with a full array of material, although nowadays precious few exist.

We store materials where we hang them. If there is any question about high humidity in your drying area, consider boxing dried material, to provide a barrier to light and moisture.

THESE TIERED
DRYING RACKS ARE
CONSTRUCTED OF
2″ × 3″ (5 CM × 7.5 CM) OR
2″ × 4″ (5 CM × 10 CM)
LUMBER (BELOW).

PRESSING

We started pressing foliage for our designs only recently. Ferns, with their interesting leaf structure and old-fashioned appeal, have become favorites for this technique.

Shrub and tree foliage are also prime candidates for pressing experiments. We have had success with oak, silver maple, sassafras, river birch, and *Lonicera fragrantissima* from our grounds. This last is a delightful plant exuding the most penetrating sweetness from its blossoms in early spring, at the time when the forsythia puts forth its yellow flourishes. We thought this was its main treasure until we discovered that the durable leaves can be pressed to an unrivaled crispness and color.

The mechanics of pressing are straightforward. Material needs to be kept flat; and at the same time moisture must be allowed to escape, otherwise foliage will curl, shrivel, or contort. We recommend a minimum of two layers of newspaper "sandwiching" the pressed material, weighted down by books, untrafficked rugs, or the like. Victorian ladies pressed their leaves in favorite volumes of literature, while modern enthusiasts use old telephone directories. Under normal conditions, leaves may be expected to dry in about seven to ten days. When dry, pressed materials can be stored in boxes large enough to accommodate your newspaper sheaths. The boxes used by fresh flower growers for air shipment to wholesale florists are ideal for this purpose. Chances are a florist will save these boxes for you if you ask.

WE OFTEN USE PRESSED FLOWERS AND LEAVES IN OUR THREE-DIMENSIONAL ARRANGEMENTS, BUT THEY CAN ALSO BE USED TO MAKE LOVELY PICTORIAL ARRANGEMENTS. THIS TECHNIQUE HAS A TRADITION OF ITS OWN, NOW BEING REVIVED IN NEW AND ORIGINAL WAYS BY CONTEMPORARY FLORAL ARTISTS.

DRYING WITH SILICA GEL AND RELATED MEDIA

An alternative to air-drying flowers is drying them in a medium that supports the fragile flower structure while encouraging them to relinquish their moisture. This method can result in strikingly fresh-looking dried flowers. In the past, sand or a mixture of cornmeal and borax (three parts cornmeal to one part borax) was used to dry flowers. There are actually many advantages to using these materials: Airtight containers are unnecessary; flowers can be left indefinitely in the medium without becoming brittle; and they are readily available and inexpensive. There is one major disadvantage, however: Drying time is lengthy—three to five weeks. The modern equivalent, granulated silica gel, requires only about one week.

FLOWERS ARE SUPPORTED FROM BENEATH, FILLED FROM ABOVE, THEN COMPLETELY COVERED WITH SILICA GEL.

No matter which method you choose, the drying procedure is simple. Unless the flowers are to be used for gluing, the flower stems should be trimmed to about one inch (2.5 cm), into which a piece of six-inch (15-cm) florist's wire (22 or 24 gauge) is inserted. As the flower dries, the stem will shrink and hold the wire securely. For flowers to be used in arrangements, the desired length of extra wire is added by splicing with florist's tape. (See chapter seven for step-by-step instructions.) Most flowers will be dried with the head facing up.

Next, pour into an adequately large container a bed of drying medium deep enough to cover the flowers. If the flowers to be dried are wired, bend the wire at a 90° angle where it emerges from the shortened stem before placing the flower into the medium. Pour medium

around and into the flowers so that the flowers are supported from below before further weight is added to the flower head. Be sure the flower is completely surrounded. You must take care to support the petals in a natural orientation so that the finished product looks genuine and unaffected. Continue to pour medium over and around the flowers until they are completely covered. Flat flowers, like daisies or coreopsis, can be dried face down with stems sticking out of the medium. Spikes containing multiple flowers, like delphinium, larkspur, and lilac, can be dried on their sides.

To test flowers for dryness, simply tilt the container until the flowers are gently revealed. Then carefully excavate using your fingers, or even better, a utensil such as a spoon or Popsicle stick. Flowers that are dry

A VARIETY OF
FLOWERS CAN BE
DRIED IN SILICA GEL,
INCLUDING ZINNIAS, IRISES,
ROSES, AND PEONIES.

are unmistakably crisp or papery to the touch. Some flowers tend to dry unevenly, however. Typically the tips of the petals may dry well while the base or calyx still contains moisture. Simply reinsert only the undried portions into the medium. Roses and other similarly structured flowers will sometimes shed petals while drying in this way. These petals can be reattached with the aid of either white or hot glue. Testing for dryness is critical when using silica gel. The lapse of a day can sometimes mean the difference between intact or disintegrated flowers.

Silica gel is available through craft, floral, and garden-supply companies. Although expensive, it is reusable indefinitely. Accumulated moisture is easily removed by heating the gel in the oven for a few minutes. Follow the manufacturer's directions for optimal results.

It is important to use airtight containers for drying with silica. Silica gel will readily absorb moisture from the air. Flowers dried in silica, or cornmeal and borax, are susceptible to reabsorption of moisture, making them fade rapidly. Therefore, airtight storage for flowers dried in this way is imperative. Putting a Styrofoam™ layer in the bottom of the container is handy for holding the wires of dried flowers.

An interesting development in drying flowers is the use of a microwave oven. Drying time using the microwave can be reduced to less than a day in most cases. Typically, flowers are heated for up to several minutes, depending on the flower, then allowed to set overnight. A chart showing the microwave drying time for specific flowers is available in a recent book, entitled *Flower Drying with a Microwave* (see Bibliography).

2

DESIGN CONSIDERATIONS: WORKING WITH COLOR, TEXTURE, AND FORM

From a bountiful harvest of flowers and leaves several can be selected which, grouped together, seem magically to create a new meaning. For this reason we invite you to look less at rules for design than at possibilities for developing your own sensitive combinations and forms.

Whether flowers are arranged in a silver tureen for the most elegant occasion, informally gathered into a basket, or tied with a colorful ribbon for a spontaneous-seeming bouquet, the choices are nearly infinite. Your sensitivity in harmonizing flowers and accessories will make each arrangement especially memorable.

Selecting Flowers, Herbs, and Grasses

Containers of dried materials in brilliant hues and varied textures become our palette for designing arrangements. These buoyant pinks and reds, with bits of baby's breath, will be used in richly patterned wreaths, garlands, and topiaries.

Working with flowers requires interaction not only between the flowers and the arranger, but also between the arranger and the occasion, person, or place for which the arrangement is made. Each design reflects both its maker and the materials chosen to enhance an event, adorn a special place, or celebrate a person. Our first thoughts center on the qualities unique to the reason for the arrangement. For instance, is it a gift to express our love for a friend, or is it something to help that friend make a life transition? Are we decorating for a holiday or creating a design to complement a special menu? Will the creation become a more or less permanent decoration on a mantelpiece in a formal, traditional

room or nestle instead on the sewing table in great-aunt Sadie's cozy sitting room? If the arrangement is for a person or life event, what are the qualities that seem appropriate? Softness, gentleness, fragility, and delicacy? Or robustness, energy, verve, drama? Or perhaps grace, fluidity, peacefulness, calm? The possibilities are endless.

Certain flowers are traditionally associated with certain events. For instance, for a wedding, rosemary symbolizes remembrance and faithfulness; the white lily, purity and sweetness; rose and myrtle, love; and globe amaranth, immortality. Flower meanings have developed throughout history, and it is intriguing to include these meanings in personal arrangements. You'll find a list of flower meanings on page 120.

At other times we look through our collection of flowers, our palette, so to speak, to see which flowers combined might visually communicate the right feeling for a person, place, or event. The fragile airiness of baby's breath along with several other equally gentle flowers seemed fitting for the Gift for a Newborn Baby (see page 106), especially when combined with pastels like softly colored pink and blue larkspur.

A thoughtful exploration of the floral material in the following pages will allow you to form some initial ideas as to the expressive qualities of different flowers. Color and texture are clues, as are size and scale. The bold, vibrant, almost brassy cockscomb celosia suggests the brilliance of a trumpet call, a quite different impression from the sinuous delicacy of corkscrew willow or bear grass. The spiky definition of the cattail, liatris, or ostrich fern leaf has yet a different impact.

Yet, as our experience has grown, we've realized that the bold and extroverted cockscomb can also be broken apart. Its velvety, rounded softness has a Victorian nuance, as do Queen Anne's lace and baby's breath. Once begun, your own recognition of subtle floral qualities and their possibilities will continue to grow, with surprising results. Unexpected materials will find their way, quite effectively, into your arrangements, and your creations will become more special and original.

(TOP) A BASKET FULL OF VELVETY CELOSIA (COCKSCOMB). (BOTTOM) THESE VARIOUS WILLOWS AND SLENDER CATTAILS ARE NOTABLE FOR THEIR INTERESTING SHAPES AND TEXTURES.

CHOOSING CONTAINERS AND FORMS

Containers and wreath forms are as interesting to discover and choose as are flowers and leaves. The ancient fragile basket from Grandmother's attic, the earthy, well-used wood toolbox from the workshop, the brilliantly colored tin can—all can be as useful and appropriate as the most elegant contemporary or antique porcelain or blown-glass vase.

For wreath bases we use a variety of materials, depending upon the feeling we wish to convey through the wreath. A flexible, gently twisting grapevine, full of curly tendrils, yields a delicate and graceful form in which to tuck the daintiest of flowers and leaves. On the other hand, a fat straw-filled wreath base provides a head start on a large, densely packed wreath such as the Jefferson's Garden Wreath (page 111). A single wire can be formed into a circular, heart-shaped, or oval wreath and then covered with Spanish moss or various herbs for a thin but well-filled form. The Spanish moss make a soft background for other lovelies. The herbs, scented and charming in their own right, are also delightful when intertwined with delicate flowers.

THIS IKEBANA

DESIGN COMBINES A

MIMOSA BRANCH AND BUTTON

MUMS IN A WOODEN SPINDLE

CONTAINER.

PRELIMINARY THOUGHTS ON DESIGNING

Having collected various materials and containers or forms, the next consideration is the arrangement of these elements. With a wreath we can be the most experimental, simply arranging flowers on the base while it rests on a table top. Clusters of flowers may be repeated at intervals, establishing a formal rhythm. This approach was used in the Wreath for an Elegant Door (page 96). Or a major focal point may be desired, as in the Scottish Wreath (page 74), with all the other colors and forms subordinate. Other wreaths are virtual tapestries, with many small details interwoven to create a delicately textured harmony. The Medieval Wreath (page 64) illustrates this approach.

Whereas wreaths offer a predetermined form to work around (and at times into and away from), arranging flowers in a free-standing container presents more choices and consequently requires more advance planning. Is a light and airy approach or perhaps one more dense and rich suitable for your intent? Or might a calm, linear design, such as the slender and spare Ikebana (page 80) be more effective? Is formal symmetry, with its sense of stability, called for, as in the Williamsburg Arrangement (page 98)? Or is robust, flamboyant asymmetry, radiating energy and movement, just the thing? You will see that style in the Informal Italian Lunch Arrangement (page 94), the Birthday Bouquet (page 106), and several others. Of all the works included in this book, the Dramatic Hanging Arrangement (page 97), carries the illusion of movement-captured-in-the-moment the farthest.

Each person has his or her own style. In our arranging workshops we've often observed twelve people, choosing from the same basic materials, use twelve quite different, yet equally valid, approaches to design. When we work with a group for a series of classes, we usually see each participant's style develop. The person who makes a large-scale, loose and breezy wreath carries that feeling to topiary and free-standing arrangements, while the person who delights in constructing a tightly detailed textural composition will probably use the same approach in other pieces. One of us tends toward a rhythmic repetition of a visual theme, and resulting symmetry, while the other usually favors developing a sense of movement flowing from and to a central focus, and consequent asymmetry. As we gain more experience, we become more comfortable and secure with what has developed into a personal style, and we chance other design options. Working in depth with your natural style is a good way to develop sensitivity to the choices of color, texture, and form most appropriate within that style. There is no need to attempt all approaches to design at the beginning. The choices you make, as you continue working, will inevitably lead you to attempt other styles as your own needs and desires move you.

We hope that the designs in this book and the thinking that underlies these designs will serve as a starting point for your own ideas. There is little here that is technically difficult. (Step-by-step instructions are in chapter seven, where you can refer to them as often as necessary.) The narrative accompanying each design will outline our thinking and decision-making process as we developed each idea from conception to completion. We hope you will enjoy the ongoing adventure of bringing your unique design sensitivity to working with flowers.

A TRADITIONAL COLONIAL ARRANGEMENT IN A DELFT BRICK CONTAINER.

~3~

ARRANGEMENTS FOR
SPECIAL OCCASIONS

In the course of a lifetime there are many events that warrant a special celebration. Some are recurring and seasonal, like the coming of spring, marking transitions that occur through the year. Some may be widely celebrated, like Christmas, or unique to a single religion or cultural tradition (although often we find that similar themes can be found in other cultures). Other occasions are more personal and private, noted primarily within the family and among close friends.

A few of the occasions we have chosen are familiar but interpreted here in a personal way; others are so seasonal and widely experienced that they sometimes pass unnoticed. We have also elected to interpret a celebration, St. Lucy's Day, most revered in Scandinavia, hardly known in America, yet especially loved by us.

Whether you attempt to reproduce these arrangements or are inspired to develop your own themes and interpretations, we hope that with the addition of a beautiful dried floral design each special occasion will take on new meaning for you and those you love.

SPRINGTIME TOPIARY

Springtime bespeaks the delicacy and tenderness of new growth. There is a tension between this vulnerability and lightness and the robust buoyancy and vitality that underlies urgent renewal. Growth suggests the use of a living form, perhaps a tree or a garden. Somehow flowers removed from their source seem contrary to the very meaning of spring. The formality of a topiary in a brass pot seemed natural. Indeed, our topiary represents a tree growing in a garden setting.

Most of our choices helped underscore a basic interaction of softness with vitality: softness of the overall head atop a sturdy upward trunk of wild cherry, the vital gleam of the brass contrasted with the sheet moss garden cascading over and thus softening the brass edges. This garden itself represents a jumble of growing forms within a calm green field, similar to the pastoral effect of medieval tapestries. The head, making a similarly delicate yet vibrant statement, is without a doubt the central focus of the design. The soft flowers and textures radiate dynamically from the center. Pastel greens and pinks intermingle with subdued shades of white and gray.

The white ammobium with its dark center adds a piquant accent. Yellow and lavender annual statice are like a savory spice—a little goes a long way. Textural variety is paramount in this topiary composition, with wild grass providing the needed filler.

Although no rules are mandatory in completing a topiary ball, this particular one was built in layers, the first being a Spanish moss covering. The next level is a wild grass filler inserted through the moss into the Styrofoam™. At this point the ball has a 1½-to-2-inch thick (4-to-5-cm) covering of grass. (See page 119 for step-by-step instructions.)

Globe amaranths, lamb's ears, pussy willow, and hare's tail grass are worked into the wild grass layer and then punctuated with spiky outcroppings of larkspur, foxtail grass, sage leaves, and wild amaranth. At this point, we felt that a fuller range of color was called for, something distinctive to act as a counterpoint to the overall softness: Ammobium and annual statice provided the "spice" to finish off this topiary.

THIS TOPIARY TREE, FULL OF THE FLORAL GIFTS OF SPRING, IS DESIGNED TO EXPRESS BOTH THE SOFTNESS AND THE VITALITY OF THIS BEAUTIFUL SEASON.

W * E * D * D * I * N * G

A wedding celebrates the joy of love and a new stage of life with warm
wishes for happiness, health, and continued joy. Tinged with the
delicacy and fragility of the new and the excitement of beginnings,
it represents the joining of what was formerly separate into a dynamic
new union.

BRIDAL CHAPLET

The bridal queen deserves a chaplet crown of dried flowers, made on
a Spanish-moss-covered wire and festooned with ribbon streamers
(see page 118 for step-by-step instructions). In this case, a merry rainbow
assortment of herbs and flowers glued in place makes a fitting statement
for all to see, in a chaplet worn from the top of the head downward
behind the ears. Many flowers and herbs contribute to this white and
pastel-colored crown. Among the whites are Queen Anne's lace, silica-
dried paperwhite narcissus for esteem, pert ammobium blossoms,
white globe amaranth, and individual bells of Ireland, a little more
on the beige side. Gentle colors come from pink globe amaranth for
immortality and perseverence, pink larkspur for laughter and levity,
nigella pods, yellow annual statice (an important addition that perks up
the whole chaplet), and jaunty pink strawflowers. The herbs are a must:
rosemary for remembrance and sage for health and long life. The overall feel of this combination of materials is very feminine and festive.

A DELICATE CROWN
OF FLOWERS FOR
THE BRIDE TO WEAR ON HER
SPECIAL DAY.

HERBAL BOUQUET

The wedding bouquet depicted here is an herbal bouquet filled with plants of particular symbolic significance. For instance, there is marjoram for joy and happiness, lavender for devotion, and rosemary for remembrance and fidelity. Amaranth denotes constancy, while narcissus lends a healthy dose of self-esteem. A most interesting addition to this herbal bouquet is pressed rue leaves, a symbol of virginity and an agent of good luck for the new household. Lithuanians, especially, are fond of employing rue during marriage ceremonies, when it is worn by the bride as well as the groom's attendants. The herbal wedding bouquet is a gathered collection of stems bound together. Stemless flowers and leaves are glued into the bouquet body, which is then fitted with a lace collar. In gathering the bouquet in your hand, maintain a constant alertness to balances of texture, color, and rhythm. We sought a dynamic tension between a sense of liveliness and a peaceful resolve.

THIS HERBAL
WEDDING BOUQUET
CONTAINS FLORAL WISHES OF
JOY AND LONG - LASTING HEALTH
AND HAPPINESS.

FIRST WEDDING ANNIVERSARY ARRANGEMENT

For many happy couples, tradition prescribes that the top layer of the wedding cake be saved as part of a more private celebration on the couple's first anniversary. Historically, the cake was a rich fruitcake, and it was preserved by the brandy it contained rather than the miracle of modern freezing.

What a pleasant surprise it would be for a couple to receive a gracious arrangement made from their very wedding flowers. These flowers were saved by a member of the wedding party who air-dried and silica-dried a selection of the finest blossoms selected from bouquets and decorations. Each tells its own sentimental story from the wedding day.

Arranged in a pewter bowl, itself also an anniversary gift, are a typical florist's collection of foliage and flowers used in fresh wedding arrangements. Exquisite lady's slipper orchids and white carnations, both silica-dried, are wired and inserted into the foam oasis, followed by baker's fern foliage and baby's breath to provide filler. Finally, delicate silica-dried paperwhite narcissus are glued into spaces between the larger white flowers.

A DRIED ARRANGEMENT MADE FROM THE BRIDE'S FRESH WEDDING BOUQUET CAN BE A LOVELY FEATURE OF HER FIRST ANNIVERSARY CELEBRATION.

ST. LUCY'S DAY HEAD WREATH OR CENTERPIECE

December thirteenth comes at the darkest, most somber time of the year. Increasing cold and darkness, especially in northern climes such as Sweden's, seem all but irreversible. Surely it must take some form of magic, a special intercession, to bring back the light that promotes warmth, comfort, and growth. Saint Lucy, patron saint of eyes and vision, must be the one to restore the healthy glow of life. In that cold season, when much is white, very few plants still hold the greenery of the past summer, yet those greens that hang on so tenaciously bear with them the hope that life endures the cold darkness still ahead.

At dawn on the morning of December thirteenth, it is the tradition in Sweden for the eldest daughter and her siblings to steal into their parents' room with special saffron bread to assuage hunger and candles to light the darkness. The light is provided by a head wreath complete with five candles. A moist kerchief protects the hair. Songs are sung to honor St. Lucy and help dispel winter's gloom.

Typically, the St. Lucy's wreath is made of evergreens and enchantingly red lingonberries, relatives of the cranberry. Our wreath is made by wiring boxwood onto a narrow straw frame fitted according to head size. Strips of tin are cut and formed into rings sized to accommodate small candles, and then hot-glued onto the frame after the boxwood has been secured. Pressed mahonia and lonicera leaves are glued into the boxwood, as are red pepperberries (our lingonberry substitute), along with a constellation of Queen Anne's lace.

It is important to note that the St. Lucy's Day wreath can very easily double as an Advent wreath or centerpiece, as suggested in the setting shown here.

THIS FINE, CANDLED
ST. LUCY'S DAY
WREATH IS THE CENTERPIECE ON
A TABLE OFFERING LUCIA "CATS,"
A TRADITIONAL SAFFRON ROLL.

HARVEST BASKET

Autumn brings to mind the heavy lushness of field grains and garden fruits, especially those that can be easily stored for use through the winter. Fall-gathered provisions seem to echo the last glory of the trees and shrubs, the warm oranges and reds carrying a remembrance of summer's warmth into the newly cool days and nights.

In contrast to the delicately growing trees of springtime, a basket of gatherings from the close of the growing season rounds out the year. The basket chosen is a traditional one, made of natural willow wands hand-harvested and woven by a local basket maker. Any basket, box, or bowl, made of natural materials, perhaps roughened by use, seems appropriate for this arrangement. This design reflects not elegance of the usual sort but rather a celebration of nature's abundance.

Filling the overflowing basket are treasures from garden, field, and roadside. Strong golden-orange colors from bunches of air-dried marigolds and curving spires of rusty red from sumac berries provide the robust colors in this arrangement. These two main colors are brought together by the intermediate orange-red of freshly opened bittersweet, a ubiquitous vine found along the roadsides in our area. Baptisia pods add a dark, textured accent along the outline of the form, while neutral shades of silver king artemisia, quaking and pepper grasses, goldenrod, and a form of rye grain provide a bountiful matrix into which are set the strong fall colors. Harvest arrangements of this kind are truly a gathering of bunches sharing a basket.

A HARVEST BASKET,
COLORFUL GOURDS,
AND HANGING BITTERSWEET
MAKE FOR A FESTIVE SLICE OF
AUTUMN.

C * H * R * I * S * T * M * A * S

At Christmas we traditionally adorn the house with the most treasured of our jewels: flowers, winter greens, and even fruit. Christians rejoice in the birth of a savior, and other traditions also respond joyfully to renewal of life, the return of the sun, and the intimation of abundance. The darkest time of year carries the promise of its opposite. A multitude of brilliant colors seems to burst forth, even though the outdoors may be blanketed with snow. Many around the world decorate the lush green of a tree with bright lights and balls, shaped seemingly by magic into fruit and flower and toy forms, and handmade ornaments of nutshells, colored yarn, and metallic paper, perhaps completing the ornamentation with silver, tin, lace, or fragile glass icicles and snowflakes.

The decorations shown here are our interpretations of the visual flavors of Christmas.

A CHRISTMAS GARLAND

Dried flowers add immeasurably to holiday decorations. Many people even place dried flowers and sprigs among the boughs of their Christmas trees. Shown here is a dried alternative to the typical holiday garland made with evergreens. The garland has as its core material either twine, rope, raffia, or straw roping. The frostiest German statice works well as an unexpected backdrop for showing off a bevy of white, green, and red dried materials. The base is prepared by wiring 4-to-6-inch-wide (10-to-15-cm) bunches of the statice together, or onto the core material, in overlapping succession until the desired length is reached. (See page 115 for step-by-step instructions for assembling garlands.) Then embellishments are glued into this base; among the possibilities are box, juniper or ferns, red globe amaranth, rose hips or sumac, and Queen Anne's lace, pearly everlasting, or white strawflowers.

A FROSTY GARLAND OF DRIED FLOWERS ON AN ELEGANT STAIRCASE ADDS TO A FEELING OF HOLIDAY DECOR.

IN THIS ROOM OF
BARONIAL
ELEGANCE, OUR CHRISTMAS
WREATH REIGNS IN BEJEWELED
SPLENDOR.

A CHRISTMAS WREATH

For a Christmas wreath, a German statice base wired onto a straw or wire frame makes for a fresh approach. A grand variety of festive materials can be introduced into the statice: nuts, cones, and pods (okra pods are great), decorative swirls of massed red globe amaranth, even dried fungus and mushrooms. Evergreens can be added fresh and will keep their green long after Christmas.

A dried flower Christmas wreath can be an especially festive project for more than one person. We had a grand time amassing red-globe-amaranth "strawberries" for the striking starlike design. After making such a dramatic statement, we couldn't resist finding big curving spires of sumac to echo the grand arcs of amaranth. Among our most joyful other additions were the spices—cinnamon sticks and star anise—and a large and interesting variety of exotic cones gathered from trees near and far. Our result may be different from the usual holiday wreath, but it certainly captures the holiday spirit.

THIS MINIATURE TREE OF DRIED FLOWERS, SMALL FRUITS, AND NUTS IS A FESTIVE CENTERPIECE FOR THE HOLIDAYS.

A HOLIDAY CENTERPIECE

As a centerpiece for a holiday dinner, we've designed a pyramid tree of edibles—lady apples, kumquats, dried fruits, nuts, and cranberries—along with dried material such as boxwood, Queen Anne's lace, rose hips, and globe amaranths. All are displayed on an ample array of glycerinized magnolia leaves alternating with pressed sprigs of lonicera. The lady apples and kumquats are toothpicked onto a Styrofoam™ cone, and most of the remaining ingredients are then glued onto them.

~4~

ARRANGEMENTS INSPIRED
BY CULTURES OR
HISTORICAL PERIODS

Travel, a film, or a work of art seen in a museum or book may provide an idea for a floral tribute. All the designs in this section evolved from an interest in our family background, a period of art or history, or from experiences we have had traveling. Several designs developed from our understanding of another culture's religion or make use of plant materials indigenous to places we have visited. All are ways of making tangible certain experiences and ideas that have in some way touched us.

We invite you to adapt our process for interpreting experiences and interests of your own. Accompanying each arrangement is a brief discussion of how the idea developed—the words, ideas, and feelings associated with each theme and how these translated into a dried flower design.

VICTORIAN WALL PIECE

When we think of the days of Queen Victoria, the qualities of richness and delicacy come to mind. We envision lively but regal purples, sumptuous velvety textures, and also the daintiness of lace. Victorian gardens were profuse, with well-filled beds and a sense of abundance and wealth. A growing middle class enjoyed its material treasures, adorning houses with gingerbread, ladies with bustles and ruffles, and parlors with plants and flowers. A home without a conservatory often had a Wardian case (today's terrarium) and fern stands.

This arrangement started simply enough with a butterfly-like structure made by securing several loops of dried grapevine with wire ties. From this modest beginning we developed a rich collection of textures in predominantly green and purple tones. The hydrangea cluster provides the focal center from which issues a cascading downward spray balanced by an upward thrusting spray. A number of elements combine to soften and romanticize the effect: sea lavender and babies breath, white yarrow, sagebrush, artemisia, ambrosia, and bear grass streamers. For starring colors we've introduced liatris, ageratum, and rattail statice in the purple range, and foxtail grass and ambrosia for green tones. Materials are either glued in place or inserted between the vines of the frame.

VICTORIAN HEART WREATH

When we think romance, Victorian comes to mind. One friend's daintily tendriled heart-shaped wreath seemed to beg to become a lacy Victorian valentine. This small but beautifully constructed grapevine heart was easy to adapt to a suggestive Victorian softness. The extravagant, curly tendrils were already present, as was the delightful bow of grapevine in the center. We chose to understate the effect so as not to overshadow the wreath's natural charms. What results is a *pas de deux* of ammobium flowers and hydrangea florets around the central focus of pink globe amaranths with an asparagus fern spray, with Queen Anne's lace enjoying an interspersed presence throughout. All materials are discreetly glued to the grapevine frame.

MODERN ARRANGEMENT

Twentieth-century life brings the excitement and rush of the metropolis, international travel for many, and the opportunity to meet and work with people of greatly varying heritages. There is the electronic atmosphere of information exchange, and the richness of choice that comes from the intermixing of peoples and values. Much contemporary art, with vivid contrasts of brilliant color and texture, and abstraction from the recognizable visual world around us, seems to reflect this new pace of life.

The saturated high energy of this modern arrangement comes from using dried flowers of uncompromisingly vivid color massed for maximum contrast. The colors were chosen to go with the print by artist Josh Fendell. The shape of the arrangement alludes to the horizontality of the artwork as well as the Japanese basket. Blue and blue-purple make an unusually rich showing with contributions from larkspur, delphinium, ageratum, blue salvia, and Mexican sage. Other colors are not overshadowed. In fact, this arrangement may best be characterized as one in which all colors clamor for attention. Oranges and reds come from Chinese lanterns, marigolds, safflower, peach globe amaranths, bittersweet, lovely red miniroses, and strawberry-red globe amaranths. The huge rose-pink cockscomb at the lower left-central edge of the arrangement is in a color class by itself, as it is in the Informal Italian Lunch Arrangement (see page 94). Yellow is last to be mentioned but hardly least, a very important color even though it has only two representatives —*Helipterum sanfordii* and dahlia. The piercing brightness and radiant presence of these yellow additions intensify every other color. Try to imagine the arrangement without the yellow to see how much more tame it would have been.

THE BRILLIANT,
CONTRASTING
COLORS IN THIS ARRANGEMENT
GIVE IT A CONTEMPORARY
VITALITY.

MEDIEVAL WREATH

Medieval cloisters were known for their beautifully designed herb and flower gardens. Considerable knowledge and wisdom about the culinary and medical use of herbs developed during the Middle Ages. Herbals were compiled and later published, and for the first time in Western art, individual plants were portrayed with a careful eye for detail. The famed unicorn tapestries, one set of which is in the Metropolitan Museum in New York, another in the Cluny in Paris, demonstrate admirably this love for the beauty of the individual plant, set into a veritable meadow of greensward.

The greenest of background material known to us, ambrosia (*Chenopodium Botrys*), provides the base of our medieval wreath, displayed here on a rustic door at Ladew Topiary Gardens in Monkton, Maryland. All of the herbs and flowers included in this wreath are known to have been grown in medieval gardens. The intention was to bring out in the varied abundance of this wreath the same love of each individual herb and flower so clearly demonstrated in the botanical detail of the unicorn tapestries. An ingredients list of materials glued into the wreath includes nigella; bay leaf; wild marjoram; pink, white, and blue larkspur; yellow and white yarrow; boxwood; rosemary; sage; tansy; and Queen Anne's lace.

Here, as in any creation, rhythms of colors and textures are developed naturally and intuitively. It is helpful to use a small area of the wreath and experiment with combinations until the right pattern emerges. Some materials look best coming straight out of the ambrosia base, while others "move" best in line with the natural swirl of the wreath. Materials should show off effortlessly and naturally and not look posed.

THE TAPESTRYLIKE TEXTURE OF THIS MEDIEVAL WREATH WAS WOVEN OF FLOWERS AND HERBS GROWN IN THE MIDDLE AGES.

NATIVE AMERICAN ARRANGEMENT

Native American peoples maintained a connectedness to the natural world that is rarely found in America today. Since we are trying to re-establish some of these lapsed connections at Spoutwood Farm, it seemed appropriate to pay tribute to the spirit of reverence for nature that is so much a part of American Indian traditions. Fortunately, a friend was able to lend a venerable clay pot from the American Southwest. The warm earth tones and strong symbolic markings presented a stimulating setting in which to weave an arrangement of dried grasses and pods. To enhance the man-nature relationship, we extended the use of natural materials to a bird's nest and bark from several river birch trees. Milkweed pods hold key positions in the arrangement. Included are not only open and closed pod forms but also several bursting pods beginning to spew forth their silken seedheads. Milkweed was an important bedding material, a sweetener, a food, as well as a healing plant for many Native American tribes. The dark and stucco-toned contrast of the container is mirrored in the arrangement. The milkweed silk, grassy plumes of reed, and pampas grass, along with sea oats, carry the lighter tones, while the fertile leaf feathers of cinnamon fern, cattails, honey locust, and catalpa pods lend a dark counterpoint. Pussy willow branches echo both light and dark tones.

A NATIVE
AMERICAN
ARRANGEMENT INSPIRED BY A
FRIEND'S ANCIENT CLAY POT
FROM THE AMERICAN
SOUTHWEST.

Souvenir Garden

When visiting friends and relatives, a secondary delight for us is exploring local gardens, roadsides, and fields. Last year, we Pennsylvanians enjoyed stays in several western states, each with a landscape quite unlike our green rolling hills. With permission, we gathered sagebrush, a new (to us) species of artemisia, fallen flowers from cactuslike succulents originally native to Australia and New Zealand, bougainvillea, eucalyptus, Mexican sage, and unfamiliar varieties of pinecones. Carefully packed and carried home, these treasures became a lifelike garden, daily reminding us of a wonderful holiday.

We did not begin with a preconceived form or theme for our souvenir arrangement. But what quickly emerged was the idea to play up the pure exotic quality, the strange and wonderful novelty, of the materials. Gradually we began to think about a fairyland, a fantasy world for small imaginary beings. We started with a moss-covered wreath and built a scene on top. Sagebrush extended the scope of the round wreath base in a dramatic, asymmetrical way. Radiating rosettes of protea provide focal points while mushroomlike outcroppings dance around a pinecone that could almost be a hollowed-out Hobbit habitat. An enchanting fawn-brown color predominates, but harmonizes with the moss green and with a condimental dash of color from the blue-purple of the Mexican sage and the red-purple of the bougainvillea. We hoped to create an effect that would inspire people to imagine themselves reduced enough in size to step into this wonderland and experience what we did when we strolled down streets among intoxicating gardens discovering an otherworldly collection of tropical flora.

A COLLECTION OF PLANT MATERIAL PICKED UP ON A TRIP TO THE AMERICAN WEST WAS COMBINED INTO THIS SOUVENIR ARRANGEMENT.

SEVENTEENTH-CENTURY DUTCH STILL-LIFE ARRANGEMENT

THIS ARRANGEMENT
DESIGNED IN THE
MANNER OF A SEVENTEENTH-
CENTURY DUTCH STILL LIFE
MIMICS A FRESH BOUQUET
REPLETE WITH
INSECT "VISITORS" (SEE DETAIL ON
FOLLOWING PAGE).

Seventeenth-century paintings convey a robust delight in the world. There are comely kitchen maids, a simple but coquettish servant girl playing an early game of jacks, sumptuous still-life feasts (often half eaten the morning after what must have been an evening of revelry), and glorious floral arrangements, abundant and in slight disarray. These representations always seem to convey a sense of beauty tempered with gentle imperfection and the movement of time, recalling the words of the poet Robert Herrick: "Fair daffodils, we weep to see you haste away so soon…" or "a sweet disorder in the dress…."

Everything, including the false stems in the colonial blown-glass pitcher, contributes to a vibrantly alive fresh arrangement look. Most of the colorful flowers are silica-dried: generous red peonies, roses, dahlias, royal irises, and even an orchid. Joining these flowers are some pressed leaves of fern, lonicera, and stephanandra as well as air-dried delphinium, strawflowers, globe thistle, rhodanthe, hydrangea, and Queen Anne's lace. Colors have been chosen to display a glowingly full spectrum to the eye. Mimicking the overflowing variety so characteristic of much seventeenth-century Dutch and Flemish art, this casually cluttered tabletop composition radiates a slice-of-life caught in timeless elegance.

A dry floral foam cork set into only the top inch-and-a-half (3.8 cm) of the pitcher was prefitted with false stems of varying thickness that protrude downward, providing a natural illusion of long stems when seen through the dusky glass. Arranging both flowers and foliage to obscure the telltale foam became an important consideration in constructing the arrangement. Flowers were chosen for the length and grace of their stems or "wire stems" were added and taped to resemble natural stems. Each flower was patiently placed in relation to every other as we carefully balanced color, texture, and spatial orientation. In a case like this, it matters little where you start. In general, heavier flowers do better lower in the composition; here, the large red peony provides the design's focal point.

SCOTTISH WREATH

Scotland is a land of craggy rocks, of acidic soil that hosts shimmering heather, of harsh waves beating against the cliffs, yet also of gentle dew upon the highlands. The Scottish people are strong and proud, fiercely loyal within a trusted circle. To those outside, the Scots' skirling pipes and tartan kilts, with steady drums and steady march, have become a stirring inspiration.

Materials native to Scotland abound in this wreath, which was designed to be dynamically wild and earthy with a thorny mystical power. White-blossomed heathers grow up the grapevine frame on both sides as wild roses seem to spill out around the central focus of purple heather that radiates around an authentic Scottish brooch. Dramatic sprays of Scotch broom and thorny branches of multiflora roses and haw-thorn leap out in opposite directions at the base of the wreath. As seen in relation to the rustic baronial fireplace, this is a dramatically large wreath, the breadth of the Scotch broom "whiskers" reaching more than four feet (1.2 m). Most of the material has been inserted between the loops of grapevine and sometimes glued for extra security. The circular purple heather arrangement is in actuality a wreath itself, hot-glued directly onto the large frame.

THIS SCOTTISH WREATH MADE OF NATIVE HIGHLAND PLANTS CHOSEN TO COMPLEMENT AN AUTHENTIC BROOCH, SEEMS DESIGNED TO LOOM ABOVE A GRAND FIREPLACE.

A JAPANESE
MEDITATION GARDEN
IS A SUBTLE COMBINATION OF
ELEMENTS DESIGNED TO
ENCOURAGE PEACEFUL
CONTEMPLATION.

JAPANESE MEDITATION GARDEN

One of the traditional garden forms in Japan is a sand and rock garden, which sometimes includes a few carefully tended plants. Many of these gardens are centuries old and are used daily for meditation. The rocks and sand are both carefully arranged to suggest the power and flow of nature's inevitable forces; the raked sand additionally connotes the flow of water moving around the rocks. If plants are included, they seem to be formed by the eternal action of wind and water. While meditating in such a garden, the visitor is immersed in the timelessness of the infinite, and lifted from the limitations of the mundane, transcending the world of everyday cares.

Making this miniature garden proved also to be a meditation: We arranged and rearranged the stones gathered from shores we visited and combed the sand with a few pine needles until the flow moved gently and smoothly. The stones, placed on the tray first, follow an Oriental tradition of grouping the largest and the next largest to represent man and woman, while a separate stone represents an approaching visitor. The arrangement implies a group in the process of forming. Just as they would in a full-size garden, here the miniature "boulders" are carefully positioned and repositioned until the right balance and tension develop. Then the sand is gently sifted around the stones, and finally combed and combed again. Only at the end, after the movement of the water (as represented by the sand) is established, are the tiny, seemingly wind-sculpted ming ferns and stems added with care, to echo the established balance.

The act of carefully tending this garden, recombing the sand as desired, can be so calming that, if the little garden is seen as a living process rather than a completed decorative object, it is a joy to live with as well as to gaze upon.

GANESH GARLAND

Ganesh, the beloved elephant-headed lord of beginnings in Hindu mythology, is the recipient of prayers when anything new is undertaken. It is customary to ask his help in removing obstacles to carrying out tasks, either great or small. This eldest son of Shiva is especially popular in southern India. The statue of Ganesh shown here is an extremely fine wood carving that originally adorned an Indian temple and is now used for private worship.

During worship, either in a temple or in a private residence, offerings of flowers or food are placed on the altar before the deity. The good-natured Ganesh especially likes fruits and sweets. Incense perfumes the air, and oil in the form of clarified butter burns throughout the worship. Flowers play an especially important role in the prayers of the numerous sects and subsects of Hinduism. Flowers such as roses and jasmine, along with herbs such as *tulsi* (holy basil) and marjoram, are given in offering. But in India, as in Hawaii, a garland of flowers is offered as an ultimate sign of respect. To make our garland for the noble Ganesh, we were advised by Sheila Rao of the Indian Cultural Center in Baltimore, Maryland. We selected a host of silica-dried treasures: roses—red and yellow—narcissus, dahlias, and small yellow button chrysanthemums. Flowers were glued onto braided strands of raffia.

THIS GARLAND OF SILICA-DRIED FLOWERS BECAME A DEVOTIONAL ADORNMENT FOR THE ELEPHANT-HEADED GANESH, GOD OF WISDOM AND BEGINNINGS IN HINDU MYTHOLOGY.

SOUTHWESTERN ARRANGEMENT

Beginning with a triumvirate of Indian corn ears and the notion of doing something Southwestern, we came quite naturally to the work of Georgia O'Keeffe, who has long been a favorite artist of ours. Her vision evokes many mysteries, whether the inner sensuality of flowers, the arid grandeur of Southwestern landscapes, or the monumental dignity of bleached bones.

We looked for materials to reinforce the strong light-dark, bleached earth-tone emphasis of O'Keeffe and the Southwest. The Indian corn with its radiating husk-wrapping suggested a circular form. It occurred to us to do a different kind of wreath, really a circular arrangement, with materials glued so as to radiate from the grouping of Indian corn. It is hard to say when in the process it occurred to us to feature an animal skull, possibly of a raccoon, found at Spoutwood. Apparently the O'Keeffe example was working overtime, as it provided a riveting focal point for the centrifugal arrangement. One final brainchild added another improvement. We had been bothered by a lack of dimension in the earth tones represented, even though we knew there was a considerable range even into the reds and oranges. The solution came in the form of something almost prototypically Southwestern—dried chili peppers. The peppers immediately added a third dimension to the wreath and greatly enhanced the rich, warm, brown-red tones of the corn, both raspberry and Indian. Other material incorporated in the sacred Southwestern circle are two forms of wheat, foxtail grass, sorghum, long pinecones, honey locust pods, okra pods, sensitive fern leaves, and sea oats.

EARS OF INDIAN CORN AND A BLEACHED ANIMAL SKULL FIGURE PROMINENTLY IN THIS SOUTHWESTERN WREATH INSPIRED BY THE PAINTINGS OF GEORGIA O'KEEFFE.

IKEBANA

Ikebana, the Japanese art of flower arranging, comes down to us from about the fifteenth century, along with the tea ceremony. As is traditional of Eastern approaches, this art form aspires less to pure aesthetic or decorative enjoyment, as is the case in the West, than to spiritual benefits. More than technique, attitude—an inner, meditative attitude—is important. This is not surprising when we consider that much of the development of Ikebana in Japan has been the contribution of Zen Buddhist monks. The idea that something as tangible as flower arranging could have serious spiritual overtones is foreign to the Westerner. The purpose is much more subtle than to impose an order on a grouping of pleasing plant material. Rather, the aim is to become so attuned, so at one with the materials, that they arrange themselves in accordance with natural harmonies. One must go the "flower's way," that is, Nature's. Humility and patience are essential. But let us not leave the impression that the flower arranger is left to his own devices to connect with the cosmos. There are many rules to be studied and assimilated, much practice to be undertaken before effortless mastery emerges. Primary among the basic rules is the "principle of three," which underlies all schools of Japanese flower arranging. Simply stated, the principle of three calls for a three-branch (or stem or spray) orientation to the arrangement, the tallest branch representing heaven, the shortest, earth, with man in the middle position. These, then, are the three realms of the universe. Man, suspended between heaven and earth, is sustained by spirit and matter. From this axiomatic starting point, styles, and configurations within styles, have been developed and codified.

We have chosen to represent a semiformal configuration of the classical Ikebana style. The heaven line of a mimosa branch makes a graceful S-curve before reaching a zenith directly above its source point. The diminished man line springs off to the left in echoing harmony with heaven. It is important to give the impression that the materials spring from the container as one organic unit. The earth line, true to its essence, is lower in the hierarchy, and constituted of silica-dried chrysanthemum flowers and leaves, displaying a denser, if less majestic, grace. The container, a wooden spindle, is not typical of Ikebana containers,

but was chosen for its naturalness and simplicity. The effectiveness of an
Ikebana arrangement is not measured simply by its decorative qualities
but for its calmness and simple grace, which inspire a respect for nature
and eternal values and engender a peaceful well-being.

AN IKEBANA
ARRANGEMENT IS
DESIGNED AS MUCH TO REFLECT
UNIVERSAL RHYTHMS AND
HARMONIES AS TO PLEASE
THE EYE.

❧5❧

ARRANGEMENTS FOR
SPECIAL SETTINGS

At times it is a place rather than an event that gives direction to our efforts. The arrangements in this section are designed for settings small and large, formal and casual. Each is intended to accent and harmonize with furnishings and architectural space. In some cases the arrangements also serve a functional purpose, such as the kitchen bouquet of culinary herbs. As dried flower arrangements have a relatively long life, it is well to invest thought and care into your choices so that they will truly enhance their location and add to your continuing pleasure.

ARRANGEMENT FOR A GOTHIC CHAIR

This Gothic Victorian chair is valued for the memories of a beloved grandmother and her home full of antiques. An assortment of cousins variously played king and queen and marched on knightly crusades inspired by such surroundings. Now a bit shaky for seating guests, this stately chair reigns as a handsome "wallflower," with an elegant arrangement discouraging the unwitting from using it as originally intended.

The elongated pyramidal emphasis of this arrangement echoes the upward thrust of the chair's ornate Gothic style. The intent is to provide a casual yet stately elegance. The fine brass container is chosen to express this as well as for its compatibility with the mahogany of the chair. Initially, Sweet Annie sprigs fill out and define the pyramidal shape of the arrangement. Next, the contrasting elements that create the dynamic interplay are inserted: feathery spikes of cinnamon fern leaves, both fertile and nonfertile, and red amaranth. Against these dark earthy spikes are placed the softer, lighter textures of wild white yarrow and, most important, hydrangea, its light green tinged with dusty rose accenting the blood red of the amaranth. At this point the effect seemed excellent in texture, but flat in color. The addition of the strong velvet-red of crested celosia lends a dramatic touch and heightens the presence of the dusty rose in the hydrangea.

THE VERTICAL THRUST AND DARK TONES IN THIS ARRANGEMENT COMPLEMENT A VENERABLE GOTHIC CHAIR.

INTIMATE BOUQUET

Many tiny corners of the house respond well to the light, surprising touch of an intimate miniature floral tribute, be it wreath, arrangement, or topiary. The guest bathroom will seem more attractive with an ever-lasting bouquet specially made for it; a dainty bouquet of lavender in the linen closet will refresh the senses, and chamomile, the sleep-inducing herb, makes an enchanting little nosegay tucked into pillowcases.

Here, the bracket shelf of a great-aunt's dresser, which perhaps originally held a delicate perfume or vial of rosewater, is adorned with a diminutive floral arrangement.

The fine blue ceramic vase was the starting point for this collection of blues, whites, and off-whites. This elegantly cool but sparkling combination seemed a natural complement to the warmth of the dresser's honey-colored glow. Special effort was made to create a slight downward cascade at the outer bottom edge of this arrangement, since we wanted to avoid conveying rounded regularity. Larkspur in two shades of blue, along with blue salvia, sea lavender, and silver king artemisia, provide the skeletal structure, which was then inserted into a piece of mush-room-shaped floral foam wedged into the narrow neck of the vase (see instructions, page 117). The "mushroom top" must provide enough of a curved mound above the vase opening to accommodate several stems. Queen Anne's lace and ammobium glued in place add the finishing touch. Notice how the ammobium, with its definite white color, pert shape, and dark center, acts as a focal punctuation to the design.

THIS ENCHANTING MINIATURE BOUQUET OF BLUES, WHITES, AND OFF-WHITES WAS SPECIALLY DESIGNED TO REST ON THE LITTLE SHELF PICTURED.

AN HERBAL
GARLAND IS LOVELY
HANGING ABOVE THE SINK IN
THE KITCHEN AND CAN ALSO BE
USED FOR COOKING.

THIS HERBAL
BOUQUET
CONTRIBUTES TO COOKING AS
WELL AS TO THE AMBIANCE OF
THE KITCHEN.

K * I * T * C * H * E * N

Kitchens, whether urban or country, stylishly modern or warmly old-fashioned, or an eclectic combination, are often places both to prepare food and to visit with friends. These two kitchen pieces combine festive grace with culinary needs.

GARLAND

Both this kitchen garland and the herbal bouquet arrangement contain herbs for cooking supplemented by some purely decorative elements, brought together in an artful interweave of textures. Although our garland is simply a wired string of overlapping bunches, we would suggest using a medium such as rope, twine, or raffia to serve as an anchor (see instructions, page 115). The gray-green foliage of rosemary, lavender, sage, and marjoram provide a subtle backdrop to floral stems of tansy, globe amaranth, wild yarrow, and anise hyssop. The peppers add a zesty bit of color as well as an interesting shape; they are glued in last.

HERBAL BOUQUET

This herbal bouquet is a chef's delight, as all are culinary herbs, and can be taken from the bouquet and used at any time. The Mason jar was chosen as a container to blend with the homemaking habits of our friend whose kitchen is the setting for these two designs. The glorious bouffant fountain of herbs in the jar contains some delights not featured in the garland, such as the chive blossoms and dill seed heads. The bouquet was simply gathered together in hand and inserted into the mouth of the Mason jar. The final touches, such as the noticeable downward spill of the herbs at the bottom edge of the design and a few last pieces inserted into the body of the bouquet, enhanced the rhythmic contrasts of color and texture. Once the bouquet's culinary possibilities are exhausted, the cook will find a treasure trove of herb leaves, spices, and peppers in the jar itself—decoratively exposed to view in the meantime.

SUBTLE TEXTURES
AND SOFTLY
COLORED HERBS WERE CHOSEN
FOR THE BASE OF THIS GARLAND.
PEPPERS AND OTHER BRIGHTLY
COLORED FLOWERS ADD ZEST.

HEARTH-SIDE ARRANGEMENT

When not in use, fireplaces may be adorned with heartwarming collections of natural materials. For this quiet study, a grouping of wild grasses, grains, ferns, and cattails echoes not only the gentle colors of the painting above the mantel, but also the lines of the absent fire. The old stoneware jug beautifully matches the colors found in the plant materials. The narrow neck of the jug limits the amount of material possible, yet at the same time makes it easy to secure stems. The arrangement is made by adding one type of material at a time, distributed evenly throughout in balanced interaction with each other. In this case the heavier plumes of grass, the sorghum, and the dark fern "feathers," were placed first for structure, with lighter spikes coming next, followed finally by the sinuous bear grass reaching out into the spaces around the base of the arrangement like spray from a fountain. Other materials include black-bearded wheat, sea oats, reed grass, foxtail grass, miscanthus, oats, and broom corn plume.

HORNET'S NEST ARRANGEMENT

This rich arrangement provides an informal, rustic touch to a brick farmhouse porch, otherwise a bit barren and missing a natural note.

Papery gray hornet's nests, the size of basketballs, are an engineering feat to behold. Made all in one season, these paper castles are filled with honeycombed workers' dwellings that surround the queen hornet or yellow jacket. Three or four of these gargantuan abodes have appeared at Spoutwood Farm over the past few years. They seem to grow anywhere —usually on a bush or shrub, but also thirty feet (9 m) up in a tree or at the top of an abandoned doorway. Usually useful only for a single season, they are often seen vacant in ghostly abandon.

We loved the nests so much we were inspired to build a rustic bouquet around one. We thought of making an arrangement for the outdoors, a captured slice of marsh or meadow. What resulted in our earthenware container was a fanciful combination of golden grasses surrounding the central nest, with ferns, greater and lesser cattails, fantail willows, giant yellow pressed hosta leaves, and Siberian iris pods.

EVEN A DISCARDED
HORNET'S NEST
FINDS A HOME IN THIS
ARRANGEMENT FOR A COUNTRY
SETTING.

A RICH ARRAY OF
DRIED GRAINS AND
GRASSES FORM THE BASIS OF
THIS FIREPLACE ARRANGEMENT
(OPPOSITE PAGE).

GRAPEVINE WREATH

This linear wreath was made several years ago of richly tendriled wild grapevine found on the edge of the woods. We formed the grapevine into a circle and delicately entwined it with a cranberries-on-wire garland, nuts, and holly for Christmas. In time, the berries dried, wrinkling into tight, dark little accents on the wiry base. We loved this wreath for its starkness, so much in contrast with the usual tendency to floral lushness. It reminded us of the inner strength, the iron will, the sturdy spine of those who first cleared land, creating fields within the forest. We decided to refurbish this wreath, maintaining the elegant linear simplicity of the original. This meant keeping all of the elements previously attached, including the holly, which had dried to a creamy brown. To complement the dried holly berries, we added rose hips. Similarly, echoing the tendril curves are bean and okra pods. Various pods and cones join the previously wired-on nuts to suggest a lively winter dance. Materials are either discreetly glued onto or entwined directly into the strands of vine.

The place we had in mind as we redesigned our linear grapevine wreath was this corner of a friend's dining room, colonial in feel. Objects of simple solemnity, made honestly but elegantly of natural materials, surround our circular assemblage silhouetted against the stark white wall.

THE STRONG LINEAR EMPHASIS OF THIS GRAPEVINE WREATH SHOWS OFF THE IMPORTANT FEATURES: BEAN AND OKRA PODS, ROSE HIPS, AND VINE TENDRILS. THE DRIED BEAN PODS AND HOLLY LEAVES ECHO THE CURLINESS OF THE TENDRILS.

INFORMAL ITALIAN LUNCH ARRANGEMENT

This fireside lunch was carefully prepared to initiate a leisurely afternoon visit with a valued friend. Having decided on Italian for the food, the friend's favorite, Italy became the theme for the table decoration as well. After the well-savored meal, the lovely arrangement becomes a gift and an enduring memento.

The brightly colored Italian olive oil container sets a festive, casual tone in keeping with the occasion. But it's the colors, especially warm pinks, reds, oranges, and yellows, that carry the visual flavor of this special feast. This particular arrangement is a good example of air-dried and silica-dried flowers combined to maximum benefit. The massive rose-pink celosia crescent helps undergird the arrangement and is balanced above with a silica-dried peony, rich red air-dried roses, and peach globe amaranths. Golden yarrow looms protectively at the topmost part of the arrangement, balanced by the silica-dried yellow and dahlia in trio with a vibrant yellow strawflower. Picking up on the reds and oranges are several more silica-dried dahlias and air-dried red globe amaranths and marigolds. Blue is the least used color, but it serves as an important foil to the warm colors. Notice how the monkshood, or aconite, with its curious flower resembling a monk's habit, and the silica-dried iris contrast with the red roses, yellow yarrow, and orange-yellow dahlia. The flowers were carefully nestled into the oil tin starting with the tallest, the yarrow and aconite, then following with those in the midsection. Finally the celosia crescent was given an additional length of stem to allow its precarious perch at the edge of the rim. Many of the single silica-dried flowers were glued in place last.

AN OLIVE OIL TIN IS

THE PERFECT

INFORMAL CONTAINER—AND

THE ESSENTIAL ELEMENT IN THIS

ARRANGEMENT DESIGNED TO

COMPLEMENT A SPECIAL ITALIAN

LUNCH.

WREATH FOR AN ELEGANT DOOR

This handsome interior door calls for a formal, even stately, treatment. No simple gathering of autumn harvest abundance will do here. Grace, structure, and rhythm all contribute to an elegant yet exuberant wreath celebrating thankfulness for a successful year.

Sweet Annie provides the base for the wreath. An unusually pleasant-smelling herb, both when growing or dried and used in arrangements, Sweet Annie grows up to eight feet (2.4 m), an amazing feat for an annual. This particular wreath was made by wiring the sweet Annie onto a wire frame. Sweet Annie will attach best to a single crimped-wire or double-wire frame. Inserted into the Sweet Annie and glued when necessary is a gentle clockwise spiral collection of wild grasses, bitter-sweet, golden yarrow, giant yellow-orange strawflowers, orange safflower, and globe amaranth as well as a generous assortment of pods and cones. Lunaria, also known as money plant, provides the crowning jewels.

THIS HANDSOME DOOR REQUIRES A STRONG STATEMENT—A HARVEST WREATH IN RICH, AUTUMNAL TONES.

DRAMATIC HANGING ARRANGEMENT

This majestic soaring space in a friend's new home called for an especially creative approach, a flight of fantasy, to bring the relaxing movement of a mobile into an airy bedroom. Taking "flight" as the theme, we selected plant materials for fluidity: banana leaves and staghorn fern, bits of twisting corkscrew willow, and feathery grasses.

First a structural backbone of the largest pieces was assembled and tied with wire for tentative, experimental groupings. Only when this skeleton was hung and viewed from all angles and studied for flow of form and movement were joints made permanent with hot glue. Then smaller pieces were tentatively added, again checking for flow. Each piece either strengthened the rhythm of visual movement or added an accent, counterpoint, or additional focal interest. To maintain the impression of flight, we kept the lines and material simple throughout the design process.

HANGING HIGH ABOVE THE BED IN A DRAMATIC CONTEMPORARY SETTING, THIS UNUSUAL ARRANGEMENT OF DRIED BANANA LEAF AND STAGHORN FERN WAS DESIGNED FOR GRACE AND MOBILITY.

FORMAL AND
ELEGANT, THIS
WILLIAMSBURG ARRANGEMENT
INCLUDES GLOBE THISTLE,
YARROW, LARKSPUR, AND
RHODANTHE.

WILLIAMSBURG ARRANGEMENT FOR A FORMAL ROOM

Williamsburg, the capital of the Virginia colony, has become almost synonymous with Colonial America. Interest in plants and gardening was widespread there. New plants introduced from native woods and abroad helped create an atmosphere of anticipation. We know that the decorative use of flowers was equally widespread, but there are few surviving examples. In the 1930s a young woman named Louise Bang Fisher, taking charge of flower arrangements for the restored buildings of Williamsburg, developed a colonial style of arranging based on eighteenth-century floral prints. She called her arrangements "buxom" and became famous for inserting "just one more" flower into her creations.

Whether in a five-finger posy holder, in a blue-and-white tureen, or in a delft brick as shown here, the Williamsburg style of flower arranging has come down to us as a richly bountiful formal bouquet.

To prepare the delft brick, tape a piece of dried floral foam in place, letting it protrude a full inch (2.5 cm) above the top of the container. This arrangement was started by outlining the pyramidal form in goldenrod; traditionally, foliage or soft, spiky filler materials work best for this purpose.

Once the overall structure is outlined, a formal arrangement such as this is built in layers. In this case we worked in essentially three layers: an innermost layer of daisylike rhodanthe, a middle layer of globe thistle, yarrow, and rose-red celosia, and an outer layer of spiky material (eucalyptus, larkspur, and blue salvia) interspersed with the original goldenrod. As in most arrangements, the larger, heavier flowers work better lower in the arrangement, while small, more delicate blossoms are better off higher. The slight natural downward flow at the bottom of the arrangement, aided by globe thistle balls looking almost like they were tossed overboard, makes for an interesting effect.

~6~
Arrangements for
Special People

The most personal and individual arrangements seem to develop as we plan a gift or tribute to a special person. While planning our floral tribute we think most tenderly about what a friend means to us, or what we wish for them at this time. In this chapter, we even include arrangements inspired by two of our heroes from other centuries, both of whom lived by values we still strongly respond to. Working from each of these approaches yielded not only a lovely design or an appreciated gift, but probably increased our understanding of the recipient.

ROSEMARY FOR
REMEMBRANCE AND
ROSES FOR LOVE ARE AMONG
THE FLOWERS CHOSEN FOR
SPECIAL MEANINGS IN THIS
NOSEGAY FOR AN INTIMATE
FRIEND.

NOSEGAY FOR A FRIEND

Giving friendship embodied in a bouquet of flowers is a charming tradition that has lately been renewed. During the Victorian era subtle nuances of affection were often conveyed through an elaborate system of meanings attributed to flowers and plants. Messages spoke of love and passion, or of grief at a perceived hurt, or simply of appreciation for years of loyal friendship.

We have a friend who calls these bouquets gaynoses, and why they should be called nosegays instead we'll never know. The one depicted here is meant to be a romantic message of courtship from a gentleman to his lady love. Herbs of glad tidings include rosemary for remembrance and faithfulness and apple mint flowers to suggest virtue. Roses, of course, are a central feature here and symbolize love and beauty. The red globe amaranth has come to mean immortality because of its enduring color. Ferns, in this case pressed baker's fern, convey sincerity. The foxtail grass and mimosa were included by our young suitor for the sensuous tones and textures rather than for overt meaning. An interesting note about the roses: Some floral lexicons insist that roses of any sort symbolize beauty and love while others signify various meanings for different types. In the latter system, the consensus for the yellow rose is jealousy and faithlessness. This will certainly not augur well if the sweet young recipient of the nosegay turns to the wrong floral dictionary. Our poor young man could be accused of sending mixed messages.

The technique for making this nosegay is simple—everything is gathered in hand except the fern (later glued in) and the stems are secured with tightly wound wire. Finally, the wire is covered with a delicate lacy ribbon and the stems neatly cut to an even length. The whole effect is one of casual elegance. Our hero could have chosen a more dressed-up appearance by putting a lace collar around the bouquet.

GET-WELL WREATH

An apple a day keeps the doctor away. A get-well wish on a sliced apple wreath adorned with healing flowers and herbs is a unique alternative to a get-well card. Not only will this gift carry a friendly wish at this time, but it may continue to restore the spirit for several years. (For this wreath, apple slices about 1/8 inch (.3 cm) thick are dried in an oven or over a wood stove and then hot-glued onto a cardboard ring that is slightly smaller than the desired wreath.)

Prominent in this get-well wish in wreath form are age-old healing herbs such as sage, feverfew, tansy, rosemary, and rose hips. Sage, in fact, with its Latin genus name *salvia*, literally means "health" or "health-giving." Revered down through the ages for its remedial effects against inflammations in the mouth, throat, and tonsils, sage has been found to contain volatile oils that soothe mucous membranes. So highly esteemed was sage of old that in 1772 Sir John Hill wrote in his *Virtues of British Herbs*, "Sage properly prepared will retard the rapid progress of decay that treads upon our heels so fast in the latter years of life, will preserve the faculties and memory, more valuable to the rational mind than life itself without them; and will relieve that faintness, strengthen that weakness and prevent absolutely that sad depression of spirits, which age often feels and always fears, which will long prevent the hands from trembling and the eyes from dimness and make the lamp of life, so long as nature lets it burn, burn brightly!"

Aside from the apple-a-day motif and the presence of healing herbs, one more salient feature must be mentioned: The hydrangea and oak leaf hydrangea florets, resembling as they do four-leaf clovers, are fully intended to bring good fortune in quantities sufficient to restore health. Other players in the visual tapestry are love-in-a-mist, roses (symbol of love and beauty), globe amaranths, larkspur, caspia, and strawflowers. Feverfew, the small cream-colored flower, is considered to be a potent remedy for migraine headaches and reputedly useful in the treatment of arthritis and menstrual cramps. The color scheme of light green and pink was chosen deliberately to harmonize with the peach-colored backdrop of apple slices.

THIS BIRTHDAY
BOUQUET
CELEBRATES DASH AND DARING
WITH A DELUGE OF COLOR.

BIRTHDAY BOUQUET

No sentimental, blushing wish shyly encoded in Victorian cryptics, this birthday spray carries its meaning in a deluge of color.

This bouquet is the result of dual inspiration—the birthday person and the quote that brings him and the bouquet together. The quote is from Johann von Goethe, the late eighteenth-century German literary giant. It is both an encouragement to the recipient to break forth from safe moorings and explore uncharted seas and a challenge to our own flower combining artistry. The quote and the occasion call for a dramatic gesture, with strong dashes of color, texture, and form. The vivid contrast of red roses with orange marigolds creates an incendiary mix. Strong additions in the purple range, Mexican sage and liatris, bring color to a bursting point. Curving and spiking forms of wisteria pods, liatris, and fantail willow, along with the interesting foliage textures of river birch and ferns, provide a dynamic crucible for the color, enhanced by the bright tissue paper and rich blue ribbon.

GIFT FOR A NEWBORN BABY

Among the special gifts often received by mothers and newborn infants are silver mugs and spoons. Although beautiful and treasured as heirlooms, they will not need to be put to practical use for the first few months of infancy. Therefore Grandmother's own baby mug, handed on to the first grandchild, carries a dainty bouquet scaled down to infant-size.

The fully rounded fan shape of this arrangement contains the herb sage thrusting outward its leaf-curls to wish good health and long life. Spiked larkspur in shades of pink and blue set the soft tones and traditionally represent the lightness and levity of childhood. Interspersed throughout are money plant (*Lunaria*) for prosperity and baby's breath for, well, babies. The larkspur and baby's breath are inserted directly into the moss-covered floral foam, with the sage and money plant glued in afterwards.

HERE, SOFT PASTEL
SHADES AND BABY'S
BREATH COMBINE IN A
TRADITIONAL SILVER BABY MUG
TO BRING BEST WISHES TO A
NEWBORN CHILD.

ST. FRANCIS' GARDEN

Saint Francis of Assisi, born into a wealthy medieval mercantile family, enjoyed as a youth all the popularity that good spirits and sufficient time and funds make possible. Fun-loving and generous, he was well known around his Italian home town, and no doubt also in France, where he traveled on business with his father. Following a spell of poor health, he was moved to rebuild a church and ultimately disinherited by his unsympathetic family.

Full of exuberant love for his god and for the gift of life, he not only founded the Franciscan order, but wrote beautifully and poetically in praise of the "Lord with all your greatness, especially Brother Sun..., Sister Moon and the Stars..., Sister Water, Brother Fire, Sister Mother Earth who...produced fruits with colorful flowers and leaves."

As one who befriended and loved all of life, Francis seems most at home in a garden, surrounded by plants, animals, and birds. We were not able to include animals in this garden scene, but St. Francis holds a small bird in his hand and stands encircled by an abundance of plant life. A mossy grove of herbs contains dusty purple marjoram, thyme, catnip, pearly everlasting, lamb's ears, flower spikes, sage, artemisia, apple mint, wild yarrow, and the bird's-nest form of Queen Anne's lace. The "wildflowers" seeming to arise from the depths of the herbs and moss are ammobium, acroclinium, and yellow tansy buttons. Saint Francis himself carries a barely observable bouquet of rosemary, moss, ammobium, and rose hips.

Miniature gardens such as this one can be constructed in any suitable basket, dish, or tray. In this case, pieces of dried floral foam and crumpled newspaper were used to create a variable surface contour on which to place sheet moss and bunches of herbs and flowers. Sheet moss makes an excellent grass substitute, but feel free to experiment with other mosses such as club and sphagnum. Notice the theme of organic abundance enhanced by the moss entwining up the basket handle, which itself lends a halo-like blessing. The last consideration in making this garden arrangement was the single-flower accents, whose stems were glued into the moss and herbs.

STANDING IN A BASKET GARDEN OF HERBS AND SIMULATED WILDFLOWERS, ST. FRANCIS COMMUNES WITH "BROTHERS" AND "SISTERS" IN THE BIRD AND PLANT WORLDS.

AN OLD FAMILY
PHOTOGRAPH TAKES
ON NEW LIFE SURROUNDED WITH
DRIED FLOWERS AND HERBS OF
SYMBOLIC MEANING.

PICTURE FRAMED WITH FLOWERS

Special relationships can be celebrated with dried flowers and herbs. An old family photograph can be the medium of new meaning. With this piece, a middle-aged son has chosen to reenter childhood surrounded by symbolic plant gestures that summarize a lifetime relationship with his mother. There is a "laurel" crown of several kinds of fern for sincerity. Sometimes the sincerity has had to weather distance, busy preoccupation, and growth pains; persistence throughout these adversities is symbolized by chamomile buttons. Next follows sage, a wish for health and a long life for the relationship. Globe amaranth underscores the desire for enduring ties. Bits of moss betoken maternal love, balanced by the austerity brought on by the struggle for self-fulfillment in both mother and son, symbolized by the thistle. Protection is everpresent in the form of juniper. All materials are glued onto the mat before framing. A special frame is required, allowing sufficient room between mat and glass, in this case close to a half-inch (1.25 cm).

JEFFERSON'S GARDEN WREATH

Thomas Jefferson, American patriot and founding father, president and statesman, was also a gentle family man, owner and operator of a sizable plantation, and an ingenious inventor and skilled architect. A visit to the restored Monticello, his beloved home in Charlottesville, Virginia, shows that he also delighted in gardens, both the terraced vegetable beds that supplied the plantation community and the ornamental strolling and viewing gardens on top of his mountain. Always one to explore and experiment, he brought back plants and ideas from his tenure as ambassador to France, developing what he called his *Ferme Ornée* (ornamental farm), a farm of both function and beauty.

In honor of a man whose reverence for beauty and practicality and dedication to improvement and graciousness we greatly admire, we designed a wreath (heroes in ancient Greece were rewarded with laurel wreaths) created from flowers, grains, and beans known from his writings to have been staples at Monticello. From the famous flower beds along his serpentine walk we have chosen to include oriental poppy pods, globe thistle, nigella or love-in-a-mist, dusty miller, bergamot or bee balm, yarrow, larkspur, button mums, plume celosia or prince's feather, and blue salvia. Also included are oats, wheat, and a single symbolic corn kernel from the field plantings. The vegetable terrace beds are represented by hot peppers, chive flowers (most culinary herbs were grown among the vegetables), and his favorite, the pea family—represented by a single dried chick-pea. Each spring Jefferson was locked in friendly competition with his neighbors to see who could bring to table the year's first garden peas. Innumerable varieties were grown as pea gardening became a mania. It would have been unthinkable not to include the pea tribute fulfilled by the chick-pea seed. Finally we felt it necessary to add reminders of the tree plantings and wild gathered materials available in eighteenth- and early nineteenth-century Virginia: sweet gum balls and pinecones, wildflowers of Queen Anne's lace and wild yarrow, and milkweed pods. All of this bounty, some twenty-odd varieties glued to a moss frame, barely begin to do justice to the gardens, grounds, and surrounding country of the gentlemanly farmer-gardener of Monticello.

A WREATH MADE WITH MANY OF THE PLANTS GROWN AT MONTICELLO IS A FASCINATING CELEBRATION OF THE GREAT AMERICAN HORTICULTURIST AND PRESIDENT, THOMAS JEFFERSON.

ᕽ7ᕽ

BASIC TECHNIQUES

At Spoutwood Farm we tend to make technique subservient to design.
Yet technique is the essential backbone of any good arrangement, and,
as with most skills, practice brings improvement. The simple proce-
dures illustrated here are the building blocks you will need to create the
designs shown in this book as well as many others of your own devising.
Very little equipment is called for; all you will need is 22- or 24-gauge
wire, wirecutters, florist's tape, a hot-glue gun (or household glue), and
scissors or clippers to cut dried floral materials.

Some techniques, or ways of combining flowers and herbs, have
endured through the ages—for instance, fastening materials to a ring
to make a circular wreath. Others, like heart-shaped wreaths or topiary
trees, move in and out of fashion. Combine materials as suits you best,
whether in line with current fashions or in your own personal style. The
techniques shown here can be adapted to allow you to combine flowers
and herbs in any form. Be bold!

fig. 1

fig. 2

fig. 3

WIRING AND TAPING STEMS

Flowers with short, broken, or weak stems can be "wired" to make them easier to work with. Wiring creates a strong stem of any length that can be inserted into a floral foam base and is much more flexible than natural stems. The rose in figure 1 has been pre-wired for drying in silica gel (see page 28). The short, bent wire that was inserted for that purpose is now straightened and extended with a length of 22-gauge florist's wire so the flower can safely be used in arrangements.

To attach the two wires, lay the florist's wire alongside the shorter wire, and, holding them gently in one hand, place the end of the tape behind them at a 45° angle so a small triangle is created as shown in figure 2. Press down the corner, and continue to wrap the tape along the stem at the same angle, as shown in figure 3, keeping the tape taut so that it spirals evenly. Wind the tape to just beyond the end of the wire, cut if off, and secure the end.

Florist tape comes in three colors—green, brown, and white. Be sure the final appearance of the taped stem blends with your arrangement. In a pinch, masking tape can also be used, especially when the extension will not show in the arrangement or when the natural stem is itself a light beige or cream color.

Sturdy discarded stems, such as yarrow, goldenrod, thin wood dowels, or cane, can also be used in place of wire to extend short stems.

GARLANDS

A garland of dried flowers and herbs is especially striking on a banister, as a frame around a window, door, or mirror, or along the mantel of a fireplace.

Garlands are constructed by wiring together successive bunches of materials. Especially for beginners, it is often helpful to attach the bunches to a base material, such as rope, twine, strands of raffia, or a heavy wire. This serves to keep them in line, and also creates a structure that is less likely to break apart.

You can either begin by preparing a few bunches in advance or make them up as you construct the garland. Using a continuous length of wire, lay the first bunch on the core material and wire around both two or three times. The bunches of material should be full enough to completely hide the base underneath. Add another bunch in the same direction, overlapping the first, and wire, continuing to add bunches until the garland reaches the desired length. Garlands can also be made by simply overlapping and wiring bunches. Wire the stems of the first bunch as shown in figure 1, and then add to it as shown in figures 2 and 3.

To finish off the end of a garland, wire on the last bunch in the opposite direction, and fill in the gaps by gluing or wiring in extra material.

Garlands can also be constructed by making two pieces half the length desired and connecting them. This approach works well when the garland will be hung horizontally because the bunches will be going in opposite directions. Again, fill in the gap where the two pieces connect with extra materials.

Most garlands feature identical bunches of materials, but you may also wish to try a pattern, perhaps repeating a group of materials a few times and then punctuating with a contrasting bunch. Alternating two varying bunches is also a possibility. Either way you can glue on additional materials at the end, especially those, such as dried peppers, that do not have stems.

fig. 1

fig. 2

fig. 3

fig. 1

fig. 2

fig. 3

FORMING BACKGROUNDS FOR WREATHS

In figure 1, Spanish moss is laid on a straw wreath frame, covering the top and sides. A wire or vine frame can also be used. Twenty-two- or 24-gauge florist's wire is inserted into the straw and, in figure 2, wrapped firmly around the moss, at 2- to 3-inch (5- to 7.5-cm) intervals. It doesn't matter whether you wire into the center or come up from it, or whether you wire clockwise or counterclockwise.

Background filler material such as Sweet Annie, silver king artemisia, German statice, or ambrosia can also be wired onto a straw, wire, or vine frame. The German statice shown in figure 3 is formed into small fan-shaped bunches and wired with 22- or 24-gauge florist's wire. Place the stems of the statice directly in line with the *top* of the frame and wire across the stems several times. The statice should completely cover and obscure the straw frame from view. The next bunch should overlap and cover the stems just wired. Keep the spool or wire pulled taut during the entire wiring process. There is no need to cut the wire until the end. To finish the wreath, insert the stems of the final bunch well under the first bunch and carefully wire.

With longer stemmed material, such as silver king, artemisia and Sweet Annie, the stems should be wired more to the inside of the wreath frame, with the tops radiating to the outside.

GLUING FLOWERS ONTO WREATH BACKGROUNDS

After you have carefully considered where you want your flowers, they can easily be glued onto wreath bases with a hot-glue gun. A white household glue also works, but doesn't have the rapid sticking capacity of hot glue. Apply glue in modest amounts to the material to be glued as shown in figure 1. A little goes a long way. Immediately affix glued flowers to the wreath (figure 2). For stemmed material glue the bottom of the stem (figure 3) and insert into the background material (figure 4).

fig. 1

USING DRY FLORAL FOAM IN ARRANGEMENTS

In making arrangements, it is most expeditious to cut a piece of dry floral foam to fit your container. It comes in brick-size blocks and is available in most floral- or craft-supply stores. Once you've cut the foam to the proper shape using a knife, a number of methods can be used to secure the foam as a base in which to insert your flowers. Gluing works well, if you don't mind getting glue on your container, as does floral tape. Because of its resilient structure, floral foam is generally easy to wedge into the most recalcitrant openings. For containers with small openings you might have to carve the foam into the shape of a large-headed cork or mushroom to secure it, but be sure to allow enough foam above the opening to accept the flower stems.

fig. 2

fig. 3

fig. 4

fig. 1

fig. 2

fig. 3

FORMING A CHAPLET STRUCTURE

A tradition dating back to medieval times, a chaplet is an elegant way for a young woman or girl to wear flowers in her hair for a special occasion. The structure itself can be a headband, as shown on page 45, or a circular crown.

To form the structure of a headband chaplet, start with a piece of straightened coat-hanger wire in the appropriate length for the recipient (about 18 inches [45 cm] suits most heads). Spanish moss is used as the background and other materials are then glued on. Begin by twisting the Spanish moss into a rope as shown in figure 1. Wind the moss rope around the wire (figure 2) and glue it in several spots to keep it in place (figure 3). Wayward strands of moss can be removed with scissors.

Bend the wire to the shape of the final chaplet and glue flowers three-quarters of the way around, leaving bare the final one-quarter on the inside or bottom of the chaplet where it will rest upon the hair. Several inches (cm) should also be left free of flowers at each end of the chaplet where it will tuck behind the ears.

We have not yet found another material that works as well as Spanish moss for chaplet backgrounds. If you do try a substitute, be sure it isn't going to break up in the hair when it is worn. When you're choosing flowers consider issues of scale, you don't want to overpower the wearer's face.

You can also make a chaplet by gluing flowers to a headband made of plastic or some other material. Either glue flowers directly to the headband or glue on a background material, such as baby's breath or German statice, first.

FORMING TOPIARIES

We make a topiary base by filling the desired container (whether ceramic, clay, brass, basket, or other material) with plaster of paris into which we insert the "trunk" of the imitation tree. Materials other than plastic, such as sand or clay, are also possible if the trunk is properly secured. Our trunk branches vary according to what strikes our fancy. Wild cherry, maple, pine, hawthorn, and corkscrew willow for sinuosity are some we have used. We save on plaster by incorporating small stones or Styrofoam™ peanut fill. It is also helpful to embed Styrofoam™ peanuts into the plaster surface to make attaching the sheet moss cover easier, because plaster is not porous enough to adhere to hot glue. A decorative background is wrapped around the base as shown in figure 1. Sheet moss or other chosen material may be glued on before or after completing the ball. The ball is made of Styrofoam glued to the top of the "trunk" and covered with Spanish moss (figure 2) held in place with tacks, short fern pins, curtailed hair pins, or staples. Just a few are needed to hold the moss in place as you work into it. The chosen materials can be worked together in a small area then spread over the entire surface (figure 3), or each kind of material can be applied all over, one at a time (figure 4). Material with stems that will not easily penetrate the Styrofoam can be glued to those with stems that will.

fig. 1

fig. 2

fig. 3

fig. 4

FLOWER AND HERB MEANINGS

Flowers have held special meaning for humankind since ancient times. It was in the Victorian era, however, that the art of applying meaning to flowers was most highly developed. The present-day revival of this aspect of floral fascination derives directly from the Victorians. Not only could messages be conveyed with a bouquet of flowers, but the manner and orientation of how these flowers were given or received could qualify the message. For instance, a bouquet given upside down could carry the opposite meaning of a bouquet given upright. A bow tied to the left gave information about the sender while one tied to the right applied to the recipient. Some common flowers and herbs and their meanings are listed here. Our sources are *The Meaning of Flowers* by Claire Powell, *Wedding Herbs* by Adelma Simmons, and *Language of Flowers* illustrated by Kate Greenaway (see Bibliography).

AMARANTH–Immortality, constancy

AMBROSIA–Love returned

ANGELICA–Inspiration

APPLE–Temptation

AZALEA–Temperance

BASIL–Hatred, token of love

BAY LAUREL–Glory

BEECH–Prosperity

BIRCH–Meekness, grace

BORAGE–Bluntness, courage

BOXWOOD–Stoicism

CAMOMILE–Energy in adversity

CARNATION–Fascination

COREOPSIS–Cheerfulness

CORIANDER–Concealed merit

DAHLIA–Instability

DAISY–Innocence, purity

DOGWOOD–Durability

FENNEL–Force, strength

FERN–Sincerity

FLAX–Industry

FOXGLOVE–Insincerity

GERANIUM–Gentility

GOLDENROD–Encouragement

GRASS–Submission

HAWTHORN–Hope

HIBISCUS–Delicate beauty

HOLLY–Foresight

HYSSOP–Cleanliness

IRIS–My compliments

IVY–Friendship

JUNIPER–Protection

LADY'S SLIPPER–Fickleness

LARKSPUR–Swiftness, levity

LAVENDER–Distrust, sweetness

LILAC, WHITE–Modesty

LILY, DAY–Coquetry

LILY, YELLOW–Falsehood, gaiety

MAGNOLIA–Love of nature

MAPLE–Reserve

MARIGOLD–Grief, pain

MARJORAM–Blushing shyness

MINT–Virtue

MONEY PLANT–Honesty

MOSS–Maternal love

MUM, YELLOW–Slighted truth

MYRTLE–Love

NASTURTIUM–Patriotism

NIGELLA–Perplexity

OAK LEAF–Bravery

OATS–Music

OLIVE–Peace

ORANGE–Chastity

PALM–Victory

PANSY–Thoughts

PEONY–Shame

PHLOX–Unanimity

PINK (DIANTHUS)–Boldness

POPPY, RED–Consolation

PRIMROSE–Early youth

RASPBERRY–Remorse

ROSE–Love, beauty

ROSE, CHINA–Beauty always new

ROSE, RED–Desire

ROSE, WHITE–Silence, Innocence

ROSEMARY–Remembrance, devotion

RUDBECKIA–Justice

RUE–Disdain

SAGE–Good health, esteem

STRAWBERRY–Perfection

SWEET PEA–Departure

TANSY–I am against you

THYME–Activity

TULIP–Fame

VERONICA–Fidelity

VIOLET–Faithfulness, simplicity

WOODRUFF–Modest worth

YARROW–War

YEW–Sadness

ZINNIA–Thoughts of absent friends

BIBLIOGRAPHY

Allen, Judy, et. al., *Flower Arranging,* Octopus
Books Ltd., London. 1979.
Although primarily about fresh flowers, has
good sections on flower arrangements in
other times and places, as well as basic
design principles that apply to all floral
work.

Fisher, Louise Bang, *An Eighteenth Century
Garland,* Colonial Williamsburg,
Williamsburg, Virginia. 1951.
How flower arrangements were made in
the early years at Colonial Williamsburg.
A classic.

Greenaway, Kate, illustrated by, *Language of
Flowers,* Merrimack Publishing Corp.,
New York.
A jewel of a book containing flowers and
meanings. Originally published in 1884.

Hillier, Malcolm and Colin Hilton, *The Book of
Dried Flowers,* Simon and Schuster, New
York. 1985.
The best single book on drying and
arranging. A creative approach, beautifully
photographed.

Joosten, Titia, *Flower Drying with a Microwave,*
Sterling Publishing Co., New York. 1986.
A recent book by a Dutch author solely on
microwave drying using silica gel.

Kollath, Richard, *Wreaths,* Facts on File
Publications, New York. 1988.
A wide variety of creative ideas; stimulating.

Mädderlake, *Flowers Rediscovered,* Stewart, Tabori
and Chang, New York. 1985.
A beautiful book about using and enjoying
fresh flowers; it calls for a renaissance in the
appreciation of the natural wonders of the
plant world.

Nickols, Beverly, *The Art of Flower Arranging,*
Collins Publishing, London. 1967.
Comes highly recommended by reputable
sources.

Ohrbach, Barbara Milo, *The Scented Room,*
Clarkson N. Potter Inc., New York. 1986.
A gracious approach to using flowers in
arrangements and wreaths as well as in
potpourri and sachets. Beautiful
photographs with brief but clear
instructional sections.

Powell, Claire, *The Meaning of Flowers,* Jupiter
Books, London. 1977.
A delightful book on plant lore and
symbolism with an extensive floral lexicon.

Preininger, Margaret, *Japanese Flower Arrangement,*
Little, Brown and Co., New York. 1936.
An excellent summary of traditional
Ikebana, the art of Japanese flower design.
Riveting black and white photographs.

Reppert, Bertha, *The Bride's Herbal,* The Rosemary
House, Mechanicsburg, Pennsylvania.
1989.
Bertha shares many creative ideas for
glorious herbal weddings.

Silber, Mark and Terry, *The Complete Book of
Everlastings,* Alfred A. Knopf, New York.
1988.
The best single book on growing plants for
drying with information about planting,
cultivating, and harvesting a wide range of
annuals and perennials.

Simmons, Adelma Grenier, *Wedding Herbs,*
Caprilands Herb Farm, Coventry,
Connecticut. 1989.
Meaning and lore for a variety of herbs
traditionally associated with weddings.

Vance, Georgia S., *The Decorative Art of Dried
Flower Arrangement,* Doubleday, New
York. 1972.
An excellent classic, still valid, especially for
formal arrangements. Ms. Vance is famous as
the person behind the arrangements for the
State Department, Washington, D.C.

Williams, Betsy, *Planning a Fresh Herbal Wedding,*
Betsy Williams, Andover, Massachusetts.
1983.
Valuable herbal lore associated with
wedding herbs by one of America's best
fresh and dried flower designers.

SOURCES

Growers and suppliers of dried herbs and flowers are springing up at an increasing rate. Here is a brief list of companies we have found to be reputable. Terms of sale vary dramatically from one to the next; write for a catalog or price list. If a company sells wholesale only, find out if they distribute to retailers in your area or under what conditions they will sell to you.

The authors, Rob and Lucy Wood, can be contacted at Spoutwood Farm, RD 3, Box 66, Glen Rock, PA 17327, (717) 235-6610. They create custom dried floral designs, and conduct tours, classes, workshops, and lectures at their farm, as well as in other locations around the country. Spoutwood Farm offers field gardens, display gardens, and a shop where original Spoutwood designs, traditional crafts, contemporary folk art, and dried flower and wreathmaking supplies can be purchased.

Alberta Supernaturals
Olds College
Olds, Alberta T0M 1P0

Australian Harvest
R.R. 2, Box 147
Perleasie, PA 18944
or
P.O. 632
Kings Cross N.S.W. 2011
Australia

Aviva Design
15100 Monterey Highway
Morgan Hill, CA 94037

The Calvert Homestead
4555 Sixes Road
Prince Frederick, MD 20678

California Everlastings
P.O. Box 620
Dunningan, CA 94937

Coast Wholesale
149 Morris Street
San Francisco, CA 94107

Countree
4573 Bender Road
Middlerville, MI 49333

Cramer's Posie Patch
740 High Ridge Road
Columbia, PA 17512

The Galveston Wreath Company
14400 Rosenberg Boulevard
Galveston, TX 77550

Hillhouse Naturals Farm
Route 1, Box 268
Wickliffe, KY 42087

Lewis Mountain Herbs and
    Everlastings
2345 Street, Route 247
Manchester, OH 45144

Mountain Farms, Inc.
307 Number 9 Road
Fletchen, NC 28732

The New Englander
555 East Uwchlan Avenue,
    Suite 224
Lionville, PA 19353

Pioneer Imports
36 Union Avenue
P.O. Box 392
Westfield, MA 01086

Raymond A. Fleck, Inc.
1139 Street Road, Route 132
Southampton, PA 18966

Tom Thumb Workshops
Route 13, P.O. Box 357
Mappsville, VA 23407

Val's Naturals
P.O. Box 832
Kathleen, FL 33849

INDEX

Page numbers in italics refer to captions and illustrations.

Photo Credits:

© Sharon Guynup: 6–7, 10, 11, 12, 14, 15, 17, 18, 20, 22, 23 top and bottom, 32, 34, 35 top, 128

© Tony Cenicola: 8

© Christopher Bain: 9, 16, 19, 21, 24–5, 28, 29, 30, 35 bottom, 36, 37, 58, 61, 72–73, 76 top and bottom, 78, 81, 86, 87, 102, 104, 106, 107, 120

© William Seitz: 38, 39, 40, 42, 43, 45, 46, 47, 48, 51, 52, 54, 56, 57, 60, 62, 63, 64, 67, 68, 71, 74, 82, 84, 88 top and bottom, 89, 90, 91, 92, 93, 95, 96 top and bottom, 97, 98, 99, 100, 105, 108, 110, 111, 112, 114 all, 115 all, 116 all, 117 all, 118 all, 119 all

© Peggy Fox: 77